University of Marriage

Your Textbook
for a Successful Marriage

Folorunso Alakija

The proceed from the sale of each book will go towards the welfare of widows and orphans in Nigeria under the auspices of The Rose of Sharon Foundation. Thank you for your donation.

www.roseofsharonfoundation.wordpress.com

Published by Ancorapoint UK, July 2011
www.ancorapoint.com; info@ancorapoint.com
+447950743517, +447931790907, +2348034022950

Indexing by Clive Pyne
Cover design by Karl Berzins
Printed in the United Kingdom
ISBN 978-978-915-734-1

Dedication

To God for calling me to write this book and giving me the inspiration to complete it. To my husband for partnering with me on the journey through the University of Marriage.

Acknowledgements

There is very little in life that we accomplish all by ourselves. This book is no exception.

First and foremost, this book is meant to give glory to God and secondly, be a source of encouragement to others. I could not have written this book without the many people who shared with me the stories of their marriages. Your courage in coming forward with your personal notion of what worked and what has not worked so well in your marriage has encouraged me to write this book. All the stories in this book are heart-breakingly true, yet the names and places have been changed to protect the anonymity of the individuals involved.

My gratitude also goes to Oseiwe Anetor, my Personal Aide, to Adeniyi Abidakun, my Accounts Executive, to Angela Joboy-James, my Admin Manager, to Shola Adama and to Johnson Ojobor, my Admin Executive, for their work on this book and beyond. I also wish to thank Funmi Ogbue and Obebe Ojeifo, my publishing team at Ancorapoint, whose tireless efforts have turned my ideas for this book into reality. Thanks to my Editor, Helga Schier, who has helped shape my words; and thanks to my design team, Karl Berzins and Louise Moe-Dean who have made the book look beautiful. My appreciation goes to my dear Dele Alakija for his meticulous review of the book.

Finally, I wish to thank my loving husband, Modupe, and my darling children, Dele, Ladi, Folarin and Rotimi, and grand-daughter, Femi, for their unconditional support and understanding for all the times I was not fully available. Their encouragement has made my work on this book worthwhile. I give God all the glory.

Thank you!

'It is the things in common that make relationships enjoyable, but it is the little differences that make them interesting."

— **Todd Ruthman**

"when you stumble, keep faith. And when you're knocked down, get right back up and never listen to anyone who says you can't or shouldn't go on."

— **Hillary Rodham Clinton**

Contents

Prologue: God's Intention for Marriage

Part I: The Ingredients of a Good Marriage

Contents

Contents

Part III: Practical Tips

Contents

Foreword

"It is not good for the man to be alone. I will make a helper suitable for him." With those words in Genesis 2:18, God declared His intention to institute marriage.

He carried out this intention by fashioning a woman out of one of the ribs of the man, Adam. In Genesis 2:22, we read "Then the Lord God made a woman from the rib He had taken out of the man, and brought her to the man."

God gave us marriage so that it could be a blessing to us and make His people happy.

Unfortunately, the institution of marriage has been under severe and disastrous attack in the last few decades. It has been said that quite a number of marriages end in divorce or just separation. The irony of the whole situation is that many divorced persons seek to re-marry. There are many marriage counsellors around and quite a number of books have been written and are still being written, like this one, on marriage. Why is it that in spite of the violent and negative attacks on it, the marriage institution is surviving and that I believe the gates of hell will not be able to overcome it? The answer to this is that marriage is of God!

What we need to do is to continue to try to make marriage all that God intended it to be when He ordained it for our happiness and blessings. This is what this book "The University of Marriage" has attempted to do.

The author Mrs. Folorunso Alakija is quite qualified to offer advice on how to run a successful marriage having enrolled in the university a long time ago. She remains in that university out of which one never passes. It is a life-long course of studies!!!

She has been married to Mr. Modupe Alakija for 35 years and the marriage has been blessed with children and one grandchild for now.

The author came from a Muslim background and a polygamous home but has become a very faithful and active Christian while her husband was born into a Christian monogamous home. After the usual teething problems of every marriage, the Alakijas, to the glory of God, have successfully built their marriage around the love they have for one another and their children.

I believe they have tried to live out God's design for marriage in their lives. The Bible gives us God's design for communication, for managing conflict, for sex, for parenting, for handling money and in fact all areas of our lives together as man and wife.

In recommending this book to you, I say for you the prayer of Paul for the Romans in Romans 15:5,6.

"Now may the God of patience and comfort grant you to be like-minded toward one another according to Christ Jesus, that you may with one mind and one mouth glorify the God and Father of our Lord Jesus Christ" (NKJV).

Very Revd. (Dr.) 'Yinka Omololu
Provost, Cathedral Church of Christ, Marina (2002 – 2009)

Introduction

In a day and age where the institution of marriage is fast becoming trivialised and dishonoured, there is dire need for resolution and divine intervention. Divorce rates continue to soar and I strongly believe there is a better way of preserving and propagating marriages other than spouses walking out on sacred vows and responsibilities. Nobody ever said it would be a walk in the park, but like every other endeavor and commitment in life, it takes a lot of grace.

I have known Mrs. Folorunso Alakija for almost two and a half decade; over this period good family values have been the hallmark of her family. I believe this qualifies her eminently to write on the subject. Mrs. Alakija aptly defines marriage as the union of two people of the opposite sex who have pledged to live together forever, with God as their witness. Following this definition we are taken on an enlightening and educative journey through the University of Marriage.

The profound truths and appropriate biblical references in this book will encourage, challenge and motivate you till your marriage becomes nothing short of incredible. Honing biblical principles with carefully selected true-life testimonies and experiences, we are furnished with rich and in-depth resources for a great marriage and a happy home. This is certifiably a manual for every married and intending couple.

Perhaps your marriage is sinking in the stormy seas of life; consider this a lifeline to a new beginning. Maybe you already have it going good, the University of Marriage will help you maintain and perpetuate marital bliss. Irrespective of where you are or what you may be experiencing, this book comes highly recommended.

Pastor Ifeayin Adefarasin
Co-Pastor, The House on the Rock and
Founder Woman-to-Woman Ministry

God's Intention for Marriage

Does anyone have a perfect marriage? Do you? If not, what are the challenges in your marriage? Are you nursing an unhappy relationship? Are you doing anything to improve the situation? Or are you just wallowing in worry and heartache?

The time has come to win back your spouse and be happy again, the way it was in the beginning. A successful marriage is not a given; it is something you can and must work at continuously. Married life is like attending a university you never graduate from. God has instructed me to write this textbook to help improve and save marriages worldwide, to teach husbands and wives how to do it right. Read on, as I have written down His words.

A marriage is a lifelong journey, more difficult yet more satisfying than any other journey you will ever take. I know, for my husband and I have taken it together.

Our relationship started out like so many others. We met at a party and fell in love. We seemed made for each other and quickly acted upon it – even before we cemented our union before God. We got married only days before our second child was born. The delay in taking our marriage vows was due to bereavement within my family. The fact that we are still together, after thirty-five years of marriage and years of courtship, with four adult children to show for it, can be attributed to a few basic ingredients no marriage should do without.

My husband and I are so close that it is as if we are parts of one another. We know each other so well; it is as if we know each other inside and out. We truly complement each other, as we both believe in diligence and hard work in everything we do, including our marriage. We are a true couple, a partnership. My husband always seeks my opinion, on any issue, no matter how mundane or unimportant, and I never fail to do the same. Some of the advice we have given each other has been excellent and some has not, but we avoid playing the blame game as much as possible. For the important thing is that, apart from God, we rely on one another for support.

Of course, every marriage faces challenges and ours is no exception, but we do our best to resolve our differences – by ourselves, without involving other people. I never fail to be the first to kiss my husband good morning, even if we had an argument the evening before. We always look for ways to make up; sometimes we simply reconnect by asking each other for help with simple, but personal things. I might ask him to close my zipper or he might ask me to button his collar. That ends it!

Over the years I have learnt not to argue with my husband. This has been a challenge, as I am usually opinionated, but I have learnt to give my opinion lovingly and respectfully. After all that is what God wants; He expects that wives submit to their husbands, and so I do. Looking after my husband has always come naturally to me. I take care of him out of love and duty, because God expects no less of me.

By the same token, my husband is a true family man, which means that the children and I have always been a priority. I know that he will always fulfil his God-given role as head of the family as best he can. The secrets of our success as a married couple have been a deep-rooted love for each other, communication, a common purse and a shared determination to bring up our children together.

Not all of the above comes naturally or as a matter of course. It is our undying commitment to each other and to our union before God that has enabled us to get through tough times and overcome many hardships. Whenever we seem to be at the end of our marital rope, we take it to God in prayer, and then carry on. My husband and I take our vows seriously and fully expect to grow old together till death do us part, no matter what.

Indeed, it is God's guidance that brought us together almost 40 years ago and that has made us the married couple we are today. For as much as we love each other, it is our love for God that has kept us together - for what God has united, man should not part.

It must be from this perspective that He told me to write His message on marriage. It is also from this perspective that I wish to impart spiritual guidance and practical tips to those whose marriages may be on the rocks. Read on, and I know you will find the strength to carry on with God's grace.

God's Intention for Marriage

1. What is Marriage?

Simply put, marriage is the union of two people of the opposite sex who have pledged to live together forever with God as their witness.

A Christian marriage should be made up of three partners: the husband, the wife and our Lord Jesus Christ. God's intention for marriage is that it be for life ("till death do us part"). People enter into the union of marriage with the expectation that it will last a lifetime, and it is possible to fulfil that expectation.

It is written that when God created the world to have shape and form, it became necessary for God to create the first human being. Therefore He created Adam.

Then God said, "Let Us make man in Our image, according to Our likeness." So, God created man in His own image, in the image of God He created him; male and female He created them. (Gen 1:26a, 27)

But without another human being, Adam would have been bored sick, so God decided to give him a helper.

And the Lord God said, "It is not good that man should be alone; I will make him a helper comparable to him." (Gen 2:18)

God favoured Adam by creating a wife for him, obviously, God considering it a good thing for a man to have a wife.

He who finds a wife finds a good thing and obtains favour from the Lord. (Prov 18:22)

God also said that he should be blessed and rejoice in the wife of his youth.

Let your fountain be blessed and rejoice with the wife of your youth. (Prov 5:18)

God commanded man to leave his father and his mother and be joined to his wife to become one flesh. As a result, God does not see two people before Him but one.

Therefore a man shall leave his father and mother and be joined to his wife, and they shall become one flesh. (Gen 2:24)

God commanded Adam to tend the Garden of Eden and, together with his helper, to procreate, multiply and subdue the Earth. This was to continue generation after generation.

Then God blessed them, and God said to them, "Be fruitful and multiply; fill the earth and subdue it; have dominion over the fish of the sea, over the birds of the air, and over every living thing that moves on the Earth."

And God said, "See, I have given you every herb that yields

seed which is on the face of all the earth, and every tree whose fruit yields seed; to you it shall be for food." (Gen 1:28-29)

Adam failed God after Eve was created. He fell from grace and from then on began to live in hardship. Every man now has to work hard to provide for his family, for man and woman had to leave the Garden of Eden where everything would have been provided.

According to Divorce.com, a website devoted to information on divorce and its repercussions, divorce is an international phenomenon on the rise. International divorce rates are at least 39%, with the highest divorce rate climbing to as many as 68% of all marriages ending in divorce. The number of marriages ending in divorce is climbing steadily, despite the fact that people try to avoid breakups. Some people try to avoid entering relationships that are doomed from the start by insisting on pre-nuptial agreements so that they do not become targets of fortune hunters. Others try to avoid a failing marital relationship by never even entering into a formal marriage, which creates the illusion that splitting is easier. Nevertheless, marriages continue to fail, and when they do, suffering follows. This is particularly hard when children are involved, for their suffering comes to them through no fault of their own.

It seems that the devil has stepped in to break up marriages, to divide and scatter the people aiming to create disunity in the body of Christ. But God wants to make a difference. He wants His children to live in unity and harmony. He wants His children to have life and have it more abundantly; He wants men to take their rightful place in the home whilst loving their wives; He wants wives to submit to their husbands while helping them fulfil their

God-given commandments; and He wants children to honour and obey their parents.

This book is meant to help us follow His wishes.

2. Has Mankind Failed in Marriage?

At first glance, marriages seem to break up for a number of different reasons, but most of those reasons can be traced back to a lack of concern for God's commandments and a lack of commitment to one another. Both husbands and wives are at fault. According to Christianconnect.com, marriage vows seem to be no longer "Till death do us part" but "Till problems do arise!"

God knows why men and women may fall; He knows what may tempt us and where we are weak, but we are not alone: in His grace He gives us warnings to guide us before we even start the decline. It is His written word in the Bible that guides us. There we can find warnings for every aspect of life, including marriage.

My ways are not your ways and My thoughts are not your thoughts, as the heavens are higher than the earth, so are

My ways higher than your ways and My thoughts than your thoughts. (Is 55:8-9)

If mankind had done things God's way, the world could have been a better place to live in, and we might not pay so much attention to or place so much blame on the devil.

We have all sinned and fallen short of the glory of God.
(Rom 3:23)

We are not supposed to conform to this world, and behave as if the secular world is the only world there is. We are supposed to be transformed by renewing our minds and by doing things differently than that which is required in the secular world. It is when we fail to do so that we fall and things go wrong.

And do not be conformed to this world, but be transformed by the renewing of your mind, that you may prove what is that good and acceptable and perfect will of God. (Rom 12:2)

The warnings above apply to marriage. We have done most things in our marital lives our own way and expect God to ratify our illegal ways; the illegal ways we take when we disobey or ignore His will. Some commit adultery, others don't respect their spouse, and yet others don't fulfil their God-given role in marriage. This is true of men and women alike. When the marriage fails because we ignore His guidance in our married lives, we quickly blame our failure on others and end the relationship, thereby breaking His commandment to be fruitful and multiply. Where two are needed to fulfil a command, and the two separate when the relationship becomes difficult, their purpose cannot be achieved.

As a result, homes are broken as the husband and wife decide to go their separate ways. The home they built together comes crumbling down as they begin to divide their children and property or, in some cases, the 'winner' takes all – as if there ever *was* a winner in a broken home. As the couple slug it out, the children are caught in between, watching and waiting, depressed and discouraged. Sometimes this has terrible consequences for the children: they may retrogress in their studies; misbehave and join gangs, take drugs or steal. They may find solace with false friends and end up in early or abusive marriages. This is not an exaggeration. When their parents' marriage becomes unstable, children all too often feel confused and fall prey to what seems to be the next best way out of their predicament. Rash decisions made out of anger, confusion or despair are difficult to undo and may shape future lives. More often than not, the troubled ways that children of a failed marriage choose are not the ways God intended for their lives.

Therefore it should be every married person's goal to get a crumbling relationship back on track, and restore the marriage through God's abundant grace. For it is every married couple's crowning achievement to have children, and it is every parent's crowning achievement to help steer them towards a bright future. This is what I call the University of Marriage – the lifelong journey of a couple for the betterment of mankind.

This is a university where attendance is of utmost importance. If you don't attend the classes, you won't pass the tests, and the chaos that ensues in a crumbling marriage will continue to rule - husband and wife lay claim to their respective rights and lawyers wade in, placing the former partners on opposite sides of the table. Tempers rise high, leading to a combative stance as the war over finances begin to rage. Everyone – husband, wife and child(ren) – suffers emotional stress, lose focus, make unhealthy decisions, lose money and become vulnerable to verbal and sometimes even physical abuse.

God wants to mend these fences: He wants us to go back to basics, to the way of life He taught to our forefathers so that it may be well with us. He has seen our suffering and that of our children, and He wishes to correct us and bring us in line with His wishes, desires and will so that we may live and love in successful marriages.

3. Who or What Can Make a Difference?

If we choose to put God first in all we do, He can make all the difference we need. However, He has given us power to choose between good and evil; He has given us the keys to the Kingdom of Heaven, and when He created us, He gave us power over everything on Earth. As a result, we already have all the tools to make a difference; the rest is up to us – to the man and the woman joined in holy matrimony.

Our respective roles have been clear from the very beginning. Adam, punished by God for his disobedience, was to till the land, thereby becoming the breadwinner. Thus his modern descendant, the husband, must work for a living to provide for his wife and children. Adam's descendants have also been commanded to care for Mother Earth, and to populate Earth, not only to ensure the survival of the species, but also to rule over all other beings that live on Earth. In like manner, Eve, punished by God as the temptress, was to help Adam to achieve his God-given goals, thereby becoming her man's prime supporter. Thus her modern descendants, the wives, must support their husbands and tend the home.

> *Then God blessed them, and God said to them, "Be fruitful and multiply; fill the earth and subdue it; have dominion over the fish of the sea, over the birds of the air, and over every living thing that moves on the earth." (Gen. 1:28)*

Therefore, the mandate has been handed down to both men and women to ensure that God's commandments are executed according to His will.

But too many of us have failed and continue to fail in our roles. Therefore, in His infinite mercy, God wishes to mend broken homes and bring back peace and succour, so that joy and laughter can resume for the world to be a better place to live in.

His teachings are simple: God wants us to go back to basics.

At the "University of Marriage", we will learn what a marriage needs for it to work, and to work well (Part I); we will learn what makes a marriage fail and how to avoid those traps (Part II); and we will get practical tips that will help us deal with and overcome typical pitfalls (Part III). As we look into the common issues affecting marriages today, solutions shall be proffered and true-life cases will be reviewed. Scriptures and prayers will top our studies, and if we apply what we have learned every day and pray, the Lord will open our eyes and help us retrace our footsteps to fulfil His true will for our marriages.

The Ingredients of a Good Marriage

The Ingredients of a Good Marriage

1. True Love

E very building needs a sturdy foundation so that it can withstand the storms to come. Every marriage needs to be set on a proper footing from the very beginning so that the storms of life do not destroy it. That foundation is love. It is the love of God and love for your spouse. Both kinds of love form the solid foundation and substance every marriage needs.

It is love that binds a family or friendship, it is love that holds no record of wrongs, and it is love that allows compassion to take control and produces miracles.

Love suffers long and is kind; love does not envy; love does not parade itself, is not puffed up. Does not behave rudely, does not seek its own; is not provoked, thinks no evil; does not rejoice in iniquity, but rejoices in the truth; bears all things, believes all things, hopes all things, endures all things. (1 Cor 13:4-7)

Love always bears forgiveness, which is a requirement for answers to prayers.

For if you forgive men their trespasses, your heavenly Father will also forgive you. But if you do not forgive men their trespasses, neither will your Father forgive your trespasses.
(Matt 6:14-15)

It is fundamental and imperative that no couple go into marriage without ensuring that they truly love each other and will do so until death. Only deep-rooted love can make a marriage withstand the test of time, because any marriage will be engaged in war from within and from outside. It is the married partners who wage the war within and against each other; in-laws, relatives and so-called friends wage the war from the outside.

Here's an example that will illustrate the war that threatens matrimony from the outside:

> Many years back, a lady got a call from her friend to say she heard that her husband had children (several, not just one!) out of wedlock. The so-called friend was amazed when the wife thanked her for the information but refused to believe it and said that even if it were so, for as long as her husband did not disclose this information himself, she would ignore it. This was over twenty years ago today. The wife never accused her husband, and to this day, the husband has never said anything. Their marriage has been solid and they have children and grandchildren. However, the wife's friendship with the bearer of the supposed truth has gone cold. Had she acted upon her rumour-mongering friend's suspicions and not applied a woman's wisdom, she would have accused her husband without any concrete evidence, which would inevitably have caused arguments and quarrels. Both husband and wife would have been unhappy and trust would certainly have

been eroded, regardless of whether or not the accusations were true. Most likely the marriage would not have survived. However, the wife's wise and calm decision to trust her husband until he himself says otherwise allowed the union to prosper, despite danger from the outside. ■

The war within a marriage can be equally damaging and therefore, as we learn from the experiences of our elders, we must ensure we look before we leap. In other words, we must differentiate between infatuation and love, and not mistake one for the other. It is advisable to pray to God over the choice of the life partner we seek. When we believe we have found 'the one', we still have to take it to the Lord in prayer to ask if he or she is indeed the right person to help us fulfil our destiny. A wrong partner in life can jeopardise God's intention for our specific mission on Earth, for your partner plays a major part in determining your success or failure in life. Samson's destiny was not fulfilled because he chose the wrong spouse: while Samson truly loved Delilah, she did not reciprocate his feelings, for if she had, she would never have handed him over to his enemies for her personal gain.

A lady Pastor recently told me her life story, which nicely illustrates the dangers of a marriage built on infatuation and lust rather than true love.

Lydia, the lady Pastor, frequently visited a friend of hers. It was at one such visit she met the friend's uncle, an engineer, who immediately wanted to marry her, not for love but for lust. Lydia was neither interested in him specifically nor ready for a relationship in general. However, her friend arranged to bring Lydia, then merely 19 years old, to a beer parlour at about 8pm, under the pretext of escorting her somewhere. There the uncle was waiting for her and grabbed her. From that point on, she cannot recall what happened, but remembers only that she eventually became herself again in a strange house. Obviously the friend's uncle had put her under a spell and abducted her.

Her family searched for her all over the village but eventually found her with him. They thought she had eloped out of her own free will, and they left her there. A while later, he called Lydia's sister and lied to her, telling her that Lydia was married to a marine spirit, and that he and a member of her family would have to take her to the Babalawo (black magic priest) for spiritual deliverance. The handing-over by a member of her family served as a good covenant to make the ritual work and to ensure that his original spell on her would not wear off. She was to wear a demonised monitoring ring and bathe with some special leaves placed in the water. Once she was through this ceremony, he quickly got her pregnant. She gave birth to her first child in November 1993. By the time she had her second child in 1999, she had become born again. Lydia's father, a devout Christian, had told her on his death bed that the Lord had ministered to him that she did not have a real marriage and that He would deliver her in His own time. At first, when the Lord revealed more of Himself to her, Lydia rejected the truth about her false marriage. Lydia's third and last child was born in 2003, and her relationship with the Lord grew. Slowly she began to question many things in her marriage, threw away the leaves and flushed her ring down the waste pipe claiming it fell off whilst washing clothes.

Her prayers intensified and she gradually found the courage to leave the marriage. First she lived at her female Pastor's house, then she stayed with friends, preaching the Word of God wherever she went and sending money to her children from God's provisions. God led her to a prominent evangelist who gave her a home, a job as a preacher, love, care and comfort. Finally Lydia has answered God's call.

Clearly, such an ungodly foundation rooted in black magic does not help a marriage succeed. In fact, Lydia's marriage was unhappy from the beginning and ended in hatred, suffering and separation. As a result, three children grew up without their mother: a situation that undoubtedly still causes them and their mother heartache and pain.

Even if a marriage begins with a sparkling of deep-rooted love, the feeling can erode over time. The demands of raising children and working to make ends meet can make a couple forget about each other and the need to find time for one another. Gradually, love begins to fade, and before they know it, they both begin to wonder what went wrong. If one is busier than the other, he or she feels left out of the other's life, so couples must continually find time for each other and not forget that their spouse need their attention, comfort and loving care.

And you shall remember the Lord your God, for it is He who gives you power to get wealth that He may establish His covenant which He swore to your fathers, as it is this day.
(Deut 8:18)

There are some jobs that keep a spouse away till late at night every working day. The husband may never see his family if the wife and children go to bed before he returns. The relationship between the husband and wife may deteriorate because she cannot stand the loneliness any longer, starts nagging or seeks comfort and attention in another man's arms.

The story of Tunde and his wife, Bola, both Christians, can illustrate what may happen if you take your spouse for granted.

> Tunde is a regional bank manager and comes home late regularly, demanding that his dinner is ready and hot no matter when he arrives. On Saturdays he is off too, without his wife and to locations unknown. On Sundays he rarely goes to church, claiming that he needs to regain his strength from a week of hard work. Of course, his wife sees little or nothing of him and his behaviour on weekends suggests impropriety. His wife confessed to me that there is no more love between them, and that the only reasons she stays with him are her faith and her children. But since God wants us to live life well and more abundantly rather than in misery, the pair needs to find a lasting solution. They need to take more classes at the "University of Marriage", as their marriage can be saved. After all, they did marry for love and have wonderful children. ■

Some marriages that start in deep love can end in deep hatred in no time. Many break up within the first few months, and oftentimes this is due to one of the greatest dangers to a successful marriage – adultery.

> I came across a case where it seemed as if a curse had been placed on the couple on the day they got married. The husband was a handsome young man with an enviable job, but his love for his wife waned so rapidly that he began dating

many women. Though an educated and beautiful young lady, the wife had to live in the village, whilst the husband gallivanted in the city. She wanted children so badly that she, too, moved to the city and tried to get pregnant with other men behind her husband's back. But she failed, and he later found out. In her frustration, she begged her husband to take her back and confessed her own infidelities completely but he found no room in his heart to forgive her, even though he was equally guilty of the same sin. They are at a crossroads! Should she carry on working in the city and move on with her life or keep begging her husband to forgive her in spite of the fact that his ego has been hurt by her infidelity? Prayers will help her find God's guidance and repentance for the sin of adultery will get her and perhaps even her marriage, back on the right track.

This first lesson has shown that only a marriage built on the solid foundation of true love will be successful. Infatuation and lust are not enough and a love taken for granted will disappear or even turn to hatred. The next lessons on the role of the wife and the husband, will teach you how it is possible to keep the foundation of true love alive and well throughout the many decades a good marriage is meant to last.

The Ingredients of a Good Marriage

2. The Role of the Wife

Tend to Your Home

Ask yourselves: What does it take to build a home? Is it beauty, charm, money, eloquence, wit, kindness, grace, virtue, diligence, reverence for God and others, cleanliness, love, obedience, trust, generosity, or submissiveness? But of course, it's all of the above, and more. The list of ingredients for a beautiful, warm and loving home is overwhelmingly long and takes the grace of God to implement.

The wife is the homebuilder, the mother, the sister-in-law, the friend, the companion, the listener, the businesswoman, the career woman, the housewife, the evangelist, the woman-of-God, the leader, the benefactor, the encourager, the helper... Is there any virtuous name that doesn't suit her?

Unless the Lord builds the house, they labour in vain who built it; unless the Lord guards the city, the watchman stays

awake in vain. <small>(Ps 127:1)</small>

To build a home requires the grace of God, but to keep it up requires the wisdom of a good woman.

The wise woman builds her house, but the foolish pulls it down with her hands. <small>(Prov 14:1)</small>

These scriptures do not necessarily refer to physical buildings; they are metaphors that speak of building a home.

Marriage is the will of God and we must work hard to seek and fulfil His perfect will, not His permissive will. To build a home requires making our marriages work, which in turn requires that we are responsible to and for our children, our families and by extension, our communities and society as a whole. For it is in society at large that the fruits from our homes end up.

A marriage is a covenant commitment; a vow made to God and the partner, an exclusive lifelong relationship. It is a threefold miracle; a biological miracle bonding into one flesh, a social miracle through the grafting of two families, and a spiritual miracle in that marriage represents the union of Christ and His bride. The woman, "the helper", has to ensure that God's will and purpose as well as God's mandate to her husband are fulfilled with her help by building her home. A woman, successful in this task, is a good wife.

Some wives are lazy, sloppy and spoilt. Some don't even know how to cook and don't bother to learn; they just want to be wined and dined. They wait for their husbands to do everything for them, to the extent of making the husband purchase even the smallest and most mundane things for the home. This type of woman is quite happy as a kept wife, one who does not take responsibility for the marriage or the family as a whole, but instead wants the husband to take care of her. In the current worldwide economic recession this is a dangerous attitude, as a good relationship requires a wife who is truly willing to help build the home by supporting the family, and where necessary, with moneymaking ventures.

There are also wives who believe in leaving all the housework, children and home to their maids and cooks who take over their roles completely. This may go so far that the husband may begin to wonder if there is difference between his wife and the maid. A smart maid may take advantage of the situation and seize power and influence from the wife. Men have a weakness for the opposite sex, and wily women can easily seduce them, which then all too often ruin the marriage. Therefore, a wife in her role as the homebuilder has to take responsibility for her home and must be in full control. For if she is not, consider the following scenario: a husband falls ill and his wife is too busy spending time with her friends; the maid looks after the husband, caring for him until his death; the late husband acknowledges the maid's services and bequeaths his assets to her the wife is left alone and without any means.

This is by no means a far-fetched scenario:

Robert Wood Johnson I, a co-founder of Johnson & Johnson, died in 1983 of prostate cancer, leaving almost his entire fortune to his third wife, Barbara Piasecka, a former maid 42 years younger than him. Johnson's children immediately contested this, claiming that Piasecka abused their father and forced him into leaving her all of his money. Three years

> and millions in legal fees later, a judge found that Johnson had been mentally incompetent when he signed his will, and ordered Piasecka to pay Johnson's children $160 million.. ∎

As shown above, it is in the interest of the good wife to tend to her home. In addition, if and when a couple are blessed with children, it is paramount that the wife and mother looks after those children properly, no matter whether she is working or not. She has to make time and strike a healthy balance between work and family, as well as between husband and children; the wife's personal social activities have to take a back seat.

Tend to Your Children

Train up a child in the way he should go, and when he is old he will not depart from it. (Prov 22:6)

Our children are our future; they are the future of our society, our nation and our world as a whole; in short, the future of mankind depends on how we bring up our children. Create the right climate in your home through the words you speak, the rules you establish, the friends you allow them to keep, the music they play, the television programs they watch, the books they read and the type of clothes they wear. While these things may seem superficial, they are all very important in raising your children well. One of the most important lessons at the "University of Marriage" is never to overlook details, no matter how insignificant they may seem.

Just as Ruth in the Bible followed her mother-in law's instructions, all children want and need to look up to someone. Therefore, be a good example for them, be their mentor and a good role model.

"Therefore wash yourself and anoint yourself, put on your best garment and go down to the threshing floor; but do not make yourself known to the man until he has finished eating and drinking. Then it shall be, when he lies down, that you shall notice the place where he lies; and you shall go in, uncover his feet, and lie down; and he will tell you what you should do." So she went down to the threshing floor and did according to all that her mother-in-law instructed her.
(Ruth 3:3-6)

As a good mother you cannot allow your children to grow up in a vacuum. You must clearly establish a set of values and rules. Do so by reading the Bible to them daily, by praying with them and for them and they will be like olive trees planted around your table according to God's promise.

Your wife shall be like a fruitful vine in the very heart of your house, your children like olive plants all around your table. (Ps 128:3)

Tend to Your Man

Do you remember that an important lesson at the "University of Marriage" is never to overlook detail? Tending to your man involves numerous details.

Cooking good food and making a palatable presentation of it has always paved the way to a man's heart. The story of Queen Esther in the Bible is well known. When she wanted the King's favour and approval so that her people, the Jews, would not be annihilated by Haman, she fasted and set up a delicious and attractive banquet for the King for three days running before she even made her request known (Esther 7). It is proper for a good wife to ensure that she facilitates the cooking of her husband's favourite meals rather than her own. It is also good homebuilding to be generous and invite others for a meal from time to time.

A man's home is his castle and he wants to feel and be treated like a king. A man wants to come home to a neat and tidy home. Ideally the woman should be home before her husband to ensure all is ready for him. A man feels good if, when coming home after a hard day of work, his wife meets him at the door with a nice kiss or peck on the cheek. She may even take it a step further and take his briefcase, newspaper or whatever else he might be carrying. A wife, who inquires about her husband's wishes for dinner, even if an employee cooks it, makes him feel cherished all the more. The wife should always serve her husband and the rest of the family before she helps herself. Even if ladies are the first to be served outside the home, at home it is the husband who should be served first, for this shows respect.

It is necessary to ensure his laundry is taken care of. Delicate clothes (underwear, socks and expensive shirts) should ideally be hand washed by his helpmate. All other clothes should either be dry cleaned or machine washed by the wife or, if applicable, by the domestic staff under her supervision. Ironing his shirts to his specifications is another vital detail. I remember that I asked my husband to teach me how he wants his shirts ironed and after some years he concluded that I was doing a better job than he ever could.

The nails of both men and women grow to replace old ones and require grooming. Many men do not bother much about the care of their feet. Wives should make it a point of duty to ensure their husband's nails are looked after. It is worthwhile to buy a set of tools specifically for him and do it yourself rather than send him to the salon, because a good wife will do a better job. A manicure and pedicure needs a guarded dead cell/tissue scraper, a natural stone smoother, a cuticle remover, a foot massage bowl, a toe/finger nail clipper and cream/lotion. I have been doing my husband's pedicure personally for about seven years. I make sure I do a thorough job so that his feet are almost like that of a baby when I finish. Usually, the salon service takes less time and care as they also need to attend to others. My husband tells me that he prefers my pedicure to the salon's. As you look after your husband, you are also looking after your own temple because God sees you together as one and the same body.

The desire to tend to these details must come from the heart. Consider this true story:

A woman once told me that she usually waits for her husband to come home before she sets up the ironing board to iron his shirts. She does this so he notices how much she does for him. This is "eye-service", done with an ulterior motive or hidden agenda in mind, and therefore it is pretentious. God is neither deceived nor impressed by any service that does not come from the heart. It is no surprise that the woman's marriage is on the rocks. ■

Laundry, manicure and pedicure are examples of a good wife servicing her husband well. A good wife is always at her husband's beck-and call. In other words, when your husband needs your assistance, you must be ready to tend to his needs, fetching this or that, doing whatever it takes to make him feel like a king. A good wife never brushes her husband off, no matter how busy or tired she may be herself. This will pay off in the marriage, for a dutiful wife will be highly favoured by her husband, which will keep the marriage alive for decades.

Your wife shall be like a fruitful vine in the very heart of your house. (Ps 128:3a)

Submit to And Obey Your Husband

It is written that God wants every wife to submit to her husband by accepting his authority or control over her.

Wives, submit to your own husbands, as to the Lord. For the husband is head of the wife, as also Christ is head of the church; and He is the saviour of the body. Therefore, just as the church is subject to Christ, so let the wives be to their own husbands in everything. (Eph 5:22-24)

God wants her to co-operate voluntarily, first and foremost out of love, respect and reverence for the almighty God, and secondly out of love, respect and reverence for her husband. The wife is supposed to obey and not argue; she is supposed to display a quiet and gentle spirit. If the wife submits to her husband, the Bible says, husbands that are not yet born again can be won for the Lord by their wives' conduct.

Wives, likewise, be submissive to your own husbands, that even if some do not obey the word, they, without a word, may be won by the conduct of their wives. For in this manner, in former times, the holy women who trusted in God also adorned themselves, being submissive to their own husbands. (1 Pet 3:1,5)

We cannot reflect on submission without a considerable display of respect by the wife. Sarah, Abraham's wife, constantly called him "my lord", a sign of respect.

As Sarah obeyed Abraham, calling him lord, whose daughters you are if you do good and are not afraid with any terror.
(1 Pet 3:6)

Therefore, Sarah laughed within herself, saying, "After I have grown old, shall I have pleasure, my lord being old also?
(Gen 18:12)

While this specific address may no longer work in modern societies, a woman of today can easily coin an appropriate name to signify her respect. This name must show that the husband is always regarded as the head of the family and second in command over us only after our Lord God almighty.

For the husband is head of the wife, as also Christ is head of the church; and He is the saviour of the body. (Eph 5:23)

Some African women respectfully refer to their husbands as the father of their first child – for example, "Tunde's Daddy" or "Papa Tunde" or "Baba Tunde" – rather than calling him by his first name.

Submissiveness and obedience go together as virtues of a good wife. God is in full support of an obedient wife.

Obedience is better than sacrifice, and submission is better than offering the fat of rams. (1 Samuel 15:22NLT)

There is a lot to be gained from obedience and a lot to be lost through disobedience, as this example from my own life will show:

About twelve years ago, I stopped going to our family church and wanted to attend another church without my husband's consent. We came up with a compromise in that we began worshipping as a family at home on Sundays rather than go to different churches. For about one and a half years, I often dreamt that my handbag was stolen through my own carelessness. No matter how much I prayed for safety or how many safety precautions I took around the house and my work place, the dreams persisted.

One Sunday morning, when I was feeling spiritually dry, hungry and empty, I went back to our family church. My husband and children immediately followed suit and none of us has ever looked back. The dreams stopped, and I have found peace again. It was after this that both my husband and I began working diligently in His vineyard for the good of the church and our diocese. Our union has become stronger ever since and it did so because I saw the error of my ways in straying from my husband's wishes.

Also, a very young friend of mine, Halima, recently gave me the testimony of her life in the many years we had not seen one another. The last time I had seen her was about five years prior, when she had just gotten married. Apparently, she had been waiting on the Lord for the fruit of the womb. At some point, the couple had taken an interest in a girl from an orphanage. Her husband wanted them to adopt the girl but Halima refused because she didn't want to bring up a child that was not theirs. Although her husband, a Pastor, was very keen on accepting the girl, his wife's disapproval made them carry on praying for their own biological child. One day, the Lord told Halima in a dream that he closed her womb because she refused to adopt the little girl. Halima and her husband immediately decided to bring her home for the weekend and the Lord confirmed His desire for them to keep her. They did, and a month later Halima became pregnant. Her baby boy and the adopted little girl interact as if they are blood siblings who now cannot do without each other.

The good wife needs to submit to and obey her husband's wishes no matter how hard it may be, for that is God's will and only a marriage built upon God's will can stand the test of time.

If the wife follows this lesson and respects, submits to and obeys her husband, the husband in turn is inclined to respect her and stay with her and their children in a true partnership.

Show Humility, not Pride

However, some wives feel too proud to submit to or obey their husbands. Instead, they look down upon their husbands for various reasons: perhaps those wives have better family background, a superior education, higher social standing, more affluence and charisma, or perhaps they simply consider their beauty a shrine at which one worships. All these attitudes, however, reflect pride and pride has always been known to go before a fall. In other words, these attitudes cause serious problems in any home, for if the husband is constantly looked down upon, he will invariably feel inferior, which even in this day and age is unacceptable for a man.

A husband I once counselled told me that his wife had never deemed it fit to apologise to him, not once in twenty years of marriage. Was it that she was perfect in her ways? Not at all, for his list of complaints was as long as my arm. If they quarrelled, she would keep malice for days or even weeks and not even offer him any food until he made up with her. Obviously, a man treated in this way might feel obliged to eat before coming home, which, in time and if care is not taken, might lead to other women taking care of him with other pleasures as well. If and when the wife later begins to feel the heat, it might be too late to retrace her steps, and her pride may have cost her the husband.

The same wife always felt that she had every right to talk to her husband as she pleased. No matter what happened between them, whether the issue was serious or trivial, she would answer back and give him the full length of her tongue. She believed in slugging it out with him for as long as it took to ensure that she had the last word. This naturally provoked the husband, who sometimes slapped her before storming out of their home to cool off. In short, the wife's verbal abuse in their arguments caused her husband to abuse her physically, creating unnecessary marital discord due to the wife's refusal to be submissive in the first place. ■

The "University of Marriage" teaches that humility, a trait of the wise, is a virtue not everyone has, while pride is synonymous with "empty drums that make the loudest noise".

Watch Your Tongue

There is power in the tongue and we are encouraged to use it wisely because it can bless or curse. Some wives are fond of cursing their spouses once they quarrel or fight, forgetting there will come a time when they make up. A wrong word spoken at any time can break a marriage apart. It is said that spoken words are like an egg which, when dropped, break and can never be put together again.

With it we bless our God and Father, and with it we curse men, who have been made in the similitude of God. Out of the same mouth proceed blessing and cursing. My brethren, these things ought not to be so. Does a spring send forth fresh water and bitter from the same opening? (James 3:9-11)

About fifteen years ago, my friend Bisi was very frustrated with her husband's infidelity. She had done everything she believed she could to keep her husband's zippers up. Bisi confessed that one day she decided to do what she would never have thought she could: she applied a curse on her husband for his infidelity, so that he would never be able to go to bed with any woman ever again. Satan must have heard her for shortly after that, her husband stayed at home, complaining about his predicament. Unfortunately, Bisi was affected, too, because not only did he not touch any other woman, but he never touched her again, either. Obviously, while the curse may have kept him away from other women, it did not save the marriage. This clearly shows that cursing is against God's will for any marriage, as it cannot improve a relationship, but instead speeds up the relationship's deterioration. As mentioned above, Bisi and her husband eventually separated. Had she instead tried to find other ways to direct her husband's straying eyes towards her, she might have been able to save the marriage. ■

The following lesson at the "University of Marriage" is meant to give you ideas on how to avoid a husband's eyes straying elsewhere and instead keep physical attraction alive and in the home.

Make Yourself Beautiful

Have you been making yourself attractive? Do you believe your body is God's temple? Do you know God is more concerned about it than even you are?

Or do you not know that your body is the temple of the Holy Spirit who is in you, whom you have from God, and you are not your own? For you were bought at a price; therefore glorify God in your body and in your spirit, which are God's.
(1 Cor 6:19-20)

The first time Jesus lost His temper was when He found the temple misused and filthy and He immediately began to clean it up Himself. Your temple, your body, must always be kept neat and tidy, attractive and presentable. The key is, make sure your body is beautiful enough to make him want to keep looking at you and no other woman. Your goal is to please your man.

Wear clothing styles that are in vogue, both with regards to inner and outer wear. For instance, when thongs came on the scene, many married women shied away from them. But thongs have come to stay and men love them, so more married women should wear them instead of allowing their husbands to "appreciate" them on strangers. If you can afford some of the latest handbags and jewellery, by all means purchase them. If you have a special occasion coming up, encourage your husband to get something stylish as a present for you. If he can afford it, he will be pleased to oblige to show his appreciation for you.

Notice that just as fashion changes, so does make-up. There was a time when heavy make-up was all the rage, but now more subtle tones are in vogue. You must be in tune with the latest hairstyles, manicure and pedicure. Keep your nails neat and painted and/or decorated, following whatever style is popular. Don't be left out. If your man stretches his neck to look at other women's bodies, make sure it will be yours he admires more.

Keep yourself strong and healthy. Drink eight glasses of water a day, exercise at least every other day, go on a walk or go to the gym. Look after your bones and joints by taking calcium and fish oil. Get enough vitamins either by eating a balanced diet or by taking supplements. Watch your cholesterol levels and have regular medical check-ups. Get enough sleep and rest to rejuvenate. These are all very important strategies for staying strong and healthy, and your husband will appreciate it just as much as God does.

If a wife follows these simple lessons and properly tends to her home, her children and her man, if she submits to his desires, obeys his wishes, shows humility and watches her tongue, if she cares for her body and makes herself beautiful for him, a marriage built on love will weather any storm.

PART I

The Ingredients of a Good Marriage

3. The Role of the Husband

Lead the Household

A man or husband must know how to rule his own household as much as his wife needs to know how to tend it. A husband may not fail in this duty or he maybe considered a failure outside the home as well.

One who rules his own house well, having his children in submission with all reverence. For if a man does not know how to rule his own house, how will he take care of the church of God? (1 Tim 3:4-5)

The story of John and his wife illustrates how important it is for the welfare of a family that a husband fulfils these responsibilities.

John had been a careless man with respect to his family life; he only cared about his career. He had five children, of both sexes, but his wife, a foreigner, had left him. She had not played her role as a virtuous wife and good mother, and by the time she left, the boys had become drinking, chain-smoking and bar-hopping youngsters. The girls were following the same path and had started dating any man who came along. None of the children were doing well in school.

In a dilemma as to how to raise his wayward children, John pretty much threw his arms up in the air in frustration and looked the other way. He began dating another woman who was sixteen years younger than him. She had been the love of his life for several years, but she had married another man, not wanting to marry a "sugar daddy". When her marriage fell apart, he tried for her hand again and this time, she accepted and married him.

It was at this point that John's life changed. His second wife took charge of his and her role in the marriage, put her foot down and saved the day. Now the children are well behaved, they have graduated with good grades, and some have even married.

While John was simply overwhelmed by his role as head of the household before his second wife came along, there are some husbands who are not interested in children or family life. They are self-involved instead, only interested in their personal welfare. Here's an example of the problems such a selfish and careless attitude can cause.

Peter and his wife had one child, a girl. Peter was a financial consultant and his wife was a nurse. They lived in a one-bedroom apartment in New York, USA. No matter whether it was a weekday or weekend, Peter was hardly at home. Sometimes work took him out of town, but more often than not, he was out with friends. For many years, he would only go home for a change of clothes. He was the prototype of an absentee husband and father and needless to say, his daughter was deeply affected by his absence. Peter and his wife eventually separated and it hit their daughter harder than anyone expected. As a teenager she came to visit us in Nigeria, yet she was withdrawn and remote. She would just sit there staring in mid-air, would not participate in any conversation and it seemed as if she was in a world of her own, far removed from everyone else. She obviously needed a psychiatrist to help her cope. When her father was asked what was going on, he simply said, "You know I don't have any flair for children and that's why I only had one." He has re-married a woman with two children from a prior marriage and has not paid any attention to his biological daughter ever since.

His insensitivity towards his family and his preference for pleasure over his responsibilities as a family man broke his marriage and ruined his daughter's life, because he did not follow God's commandment of loving his wife.

Husbands, love your wives, just as Christ also loved the church and gave Himself for her. (Eph 5:25)

When he felt their relationship deteriorating, he did not, as is his duty as head of the household, try to save the relationship; instead he ignored his wife and his daughter and therefore failed to provide for the spiritual welfare of his family – and thus of himself.

So husbands ought to love their own wives as their own bodies; he who loves his wife loves himself. (Eph 5:28)

If he knew that he did not care for children, he should either have told his wife from the start, or not gotten married at all. For, as was said before, it is the crowning experience of every marriage to bring forth a child. Any husband and father who does not realise this, fails in his role as head of the household.

Honour, Praise and Please Your Wife

As much as any wife must honour and obey her husband, any husband must honour, praise and please his wife, otherwise, God will not answer his prayers.

Husbands, likewise, dwell with them with understanding, giving honour to the wife, as to the weaker vessel, and as being heirs together of the grace of life, that your prayers may not be hindered. (1 Pet 3:7)

A husband must honour his wife by showing her respect and letting her know she is important in his life and that he can't really get along without her. He must always speak to her politely and with respect. In the olden days, men would open car doors for women, give up their seats when seats were scarce, make room and give way for them when caught in a tight corner, and men would even get into fist fights if necessary to protect her honour, whether they knew her or not. These were ways for men to honour women generally and it was expected that such honour be extended to their wives at home as well.

Her children rise up and call her blessed; her husband also, and he praises her. (Prov 31:28)

A husband should always let his wife know how much he appreciates her for the labour of love he knows she performs for him and the children, for her support, for her advice and loving kindness. He should praise her in her presence and behind her back.

But he who is married cares about the things of the world – how he may please his wife. (1 Cor 7:33)

A husband must care for his wife's welfare and pleasure as much as he cares for his own; or, phrased differently, the husband must treat his wife the way he, too, wants to be treated.

Therefore, whatever you want men to do to you, do also to them, for this is the law and the Prophets. (Matt. 7:12)

May all men take with them this lesson of the "University of Marriage": only if both husband and wife are happy, will the marital union survive and create healthy children. As much as it is the wife's job as homebuilder, it is the husband's job as the head of the household to look out for the success of the union before God.

Guide Your Family's Spiritual Journey

Therefore, just as the church is subject to Christ, so let the wives be to their own husbands in everything. (Eph 5:24)

Not only is the husband called upon to make sure his house is in order physically, he is also called upon to lead his family in daily devotion to God. The home must provide a vital, living example of true Christianity, for it is only then that God will dwell in that home.

Again I say to you that if two of you agree on earth concerning anything that they ask, it will be done for them by My Father in heaven. For where two or three are gathered together in My name, I am there in the midst of them. (Matt. 18:19-20)

God has called the husband to be the spiritual leader of his household.

For the husband is head of the wife, as also Christ is head of the church; and He is the Saviour of the body. Therefore, just as the church is subject to Christ, so let the wives be to their own husbands in everything. (Eph 5:23-24)

The husband must provide spiritual leadership, and make sure that the wife sets up a time for daily family prayer and Bible reading, for children must be taught to talk to God about everything. This open dialogue with God creates a spiritual heritage that functions like a wall of security and protection around the house, reaching well past the physical home.

In short, another simple lesson at the "University of Marriage" is that if the husband leads with love and by example, God will hear his prayers, and his wife will respond with respect, admiration and submission.

Protect and Provide For Your Family

Every husband has to protect his wife and children from any form of danger whether internal or external. A family left to its own devices is vulnerable to abuse or attacks at any time, day or night, as the world continues to be unsafe and dangerous. Sexual predators, maniacs, murderers, thieves, kidnappers, rapists, fraudsters, fake marketers and mad men prey on vulnerable people.

Sadly there is nothing more vulnerable than a woman and child who have been abandoned by a careless man.

As much as he must protect his wife and children, the husband must also provide for his family. He must ensure that they have enough to eat and drink, adequate shelter, and clothes on their backs. Obviously, as the children grow, he has to keep changing their clothes, and he must enable his wife to meet the fashion standard of her peers in their society. He must pay his children's school fees and give his wife an allowance that adequately sustains his household.

But if anyone does not provide for his own, and especially for those of his household, he has denied the faith and is worse than an unbeliever. (1 Tim 5:8)

Though the wife is to be the husband's helper, she was not called upon to take over his role as the family's protector or provider or she will be overwhelmed with too many responsibilities. This is another 'going-back-to-basics' lesson at the "University of Marriage".

Pay Attention to Your Family

A husband and father must never take a backseat role within his family or he will fail God and them. He must not be an absentee leader, but instead he must find time to be with his wife, do fun things with her as they used to when they were courting. It helps a marriage to go to a movie once in a while, to go on a drive, to go to dinner or parties, or to take holidays together. Even simple things are important, such as telling her he loves her once in a while, making a compliment on a new dress or a fresh hairstyle, buying her presents for special occasions, surprising her from time to time and always remembering her birthday and Valentine's Day. She must have access to whatever he considers as his choice possessions such as his cars, electronics and other gadgets, and generally share things with her. All these are small ideas to make sure the husband does not take his wife for granted.

Likewise, if they have children, no matter how busy he is, the father must find a way to spend time with his children and show them he cares about them. He should play with them, take them out to the playground or sports events, find out how they are doing in school and get to know their friends.

Lovemaking is a prerequisite of marriage and must be encouraged, even after children and the stresses of childrearing have entered the picture. Not only must a wife be available to her husband in bed, a husband must also please his wife for a marriage to work. It is one of God's basic rules of holy matrimony and a lesson at the "University of Marriage": a healthy love life will bring contentment and make sure she won't check whether the grass is greener on the other side.

My own marriage illustrates this quite nicely.

I praise God that the husband He has given me appreciates and loves me and tells me so regularly. Sometimes he sends me love messages and adds a heart-shaped sign at the end. He honours me and always treats me politely. Do not get me wrong, he still gets upset with me and tells me off when he feels the need, but he avoids doing it in the presence of others, and he never does it in the presence of staff. I know that some husbands abuse their power and enjoy displaying their superiority by doing the exact opposite.

I remember a situation during the first year of our marriage thirty-five years ago, when my husband told me he wanted to go abroad on a short holiday. I told him we needed a deep freezer and that I did not think it would be a good idea if he spent money on a holiday before purchasing necessary equipment for the home. He immediately saw my point, did not argue and pleased me by providing the freezer before he left. Everybody was happy. He did not, does not and will never shirk his responsibilities to the children or me. He would rather buy just a pair of socks for himself and bring us suitcases laden with goodies.

Moreover, no matter how much we argue or quarrel, he has never slapped or beaten me. Rather than that, he would fight *for* me. I remember an incident years back at a burial ceremony. Chairs and tables had been arranged under canopies parallel to the street and all the chairs had become dusty. Before I sat down, I took the paper napkin in the drinks glass meant for me and wiped my seat. A steward who had been setting the table came running along to tell me off. Unfortunately, my husband had been looking the other way, but as soon as I told him what had just happened, he ran after the steward and told him off strongly for being rude to me. I was pleased and felt honoured, for it was a clear sign he appreciates me and won't allow anyone to insult me. ■

As much as the "University of Marriage" teaches you to pay attention to your family, the flipside of that coin is that you must never abuse your power over your family. There are many husbands who do as they please just because they are the head of the family. They assume that because they are physically stronger, they can get away with anything, even murder. There are those who torment and torture their wives and children, those who slap and beat their wives and take out their frustrations on them. There are those who rape their children and the children from their wives' previous marriages.

While these are extreme cases, abuse comes in various forms. It is a form of abuse if a husband shirks his responsibilities by withholding house-keeping money. It is a form of abuse if a husband spends his income on girlfriends and prostitutes instead of his family. It is a form of abuse if a husband spends his money on himself, buying cars, drinking or just simply gambling all his money away. Some prefer to make donations in public to earn themselves good names and be people pleasers at the expense of their families. It is a form of abuse if a husband never has time for his spouse or his children and ignores his family, believing that wives should remain in the kitchen and children should never be seen or heard.

Men can learn from Lolade's report below about the ways her husband shirked his responsibilities, and thus ruined their marriage.

Lolade complained about how her husband never wanted to take financial responsibility for his family. Even at a time when neither of them was working, he expected her to provide money whenever it was needed! One day when the couple were off to visit his father, they realised they were low on fuel, and they turned into a petrol station for a few litres of petrol. When it was time to pay, her husband searched for money that he knew he didn't have and suddenly turned to her for a bailout. She, too, searched her bag and there was nothing. He started screaming at her and telling her off. For the first time ever, she burst into a stream of objections and complaints about him, because she could no longer take the ill treatment he was meting out to her. When the petrol attendant saw what was going on, he waved them off and they left. On arrival at the house, Lolade's husband complained bitterly to his father about his wife, blaming her for a number of completely untrue incidents and semi-fabricated mishaps that demonised her and made him look like a saint in comparison.

Lolade decided to tell her side of what had been going on. Though she gave an account of the truth, the whole truth and nothing but the truth as she had been brought up to do, her father-in-law's first question was, "Lolade, how many times does your husband beat you in a year?" She answered, "Roughly about five times a year." Her father-in-law nodded in approval and then said to his son, "Well, you see, a woman must be beaten regularly to keep her in check or she will get out of hand!"

Lolade was shocked and couldn't believe she had heard things correctly. Her husband had just won another battle. She felt utterly alone and did not know where to turn.

She was providing for the family as her husband's business was not doing well, but in spite of that he seemed to resent her and he abused her physically on several occasions, often stopped speaking to her at all, and spoke to the children only if and when necessary. Her husband had extra-marital affairs, which were common knowledge, and although he couldn't prove it, he always suspected his wife of doing the same. After many years of trying to keep up appearances, Lolade felt she couldn't take the suffering any longer and began to rebel by answering back. To her husband, this was the height of insult and he walked out of their home. ■

Neither Lolade nor her husband heeded God's will and consequently the marriage fell apart. Had Lolade submitted to and obeyed her husband, and had he taken care of his wife and family as he should, the marriage could have survived.

Be Your Wife's Handyman

When the drainpipe is blocked, it is ideal if the husband attempts to fix it with a "do it yourself" guide before calling in an expensive plumber. The husband should always see to minor electrical or carpentry jobs and generator repairs to provide emergency lighting. A lazy or absentee husband will keep his family twiddling their thumbs and put them at the mercy of the many shylock handymen before things can get back to normal. So, the husband should ensure he makes himself available to play his part as and when necessary.

Husbands who do not play their God-given role are obviously responsible for a share of unhappiness within the home that could lead to arguments and fighting that in turn could lead to separation or even divorce. However, as God guards the institution of marriage jealously, not wanting them to fall apart so that families can have life and have it more abundantly and so that humans can continue to populate the Earth and worship Him to His glory, it is a man's responsibility to play his role in the marriage and household.

Just as Christ is the Head of the Church, so is the husband the head of the family. The role that Christ plays in the Church has been put in the hands of husbands; he is to love, protect, and provide for his family; he is to be ever-present, representing Christ in his home. He must guide and guard his wife and children physically and spiritually. His attention to their needs must be paramount on his mind. He must always make himself available and be loving towards his wife and children. He must not take his wife for granted but must pay her the attention she deserves; he must not ignore her, but share intimacy with her from time to time to keep the flame of love burning.

If a husband follows these simple lessons he will bring blessing, happiness and stability into his home. A husband who honours and respects his wife and a wife who honours and obeys her husband will form a partnership for life.

4. A True Partnership Between Husband And Wife

It is easy to speak of forming a true partnership when a marriage is young and love is fresh and deep. Yet over the years it takes hard work to ensure that the marriage survives.

Commitment And Strength of Purpose

Both husband and wife must be committed to one another. They must have a united front and work towards a common goal. For strength of purpose, the wife must support her husband in accomplishing God's purpose in his life.

They must be determined that from the first day of their marriage, no matter what happens, the marital vows they took must hold until death part them. The written oath that is also spoken at virtually all wedding ceremonies must be forever embedded in their hearts. They both have to take their marriage to the Lord in prayer:

1. Tell God your desire to be committed to one another for life and that you do not divorce one another.

2. Pray for mutual consent in all your endeavours. The Bible says that two people cannot live together unless they are in agreement.

Again I say to you that if two of you agree on earth concerning anything that they ask, it will be done for them by My Father in heaven. For where two or more are gathered together in My name, I am there in the midst of them.
(Matt. 18:19-20)

3. Pray against any form of unfaithfulness or adultery that could cause a separation or divorce.

You shall not commit adultery. (Matt. 5:27b)

Nevertheless, because of sexual immorality, let each man have his own wife, and let each woman have her own husband. Let the husband render to his wife the affection due her, and likewise also the wife to her husband. (1 Cor 7:2-3)

4.   Speak to God and ask Him to protect your marriage from evil coming from outsiders and in-laws.

5.   Ask God to strengthen you both to never to give in or give up on your marriage, even if the going should get tough.

The "University of Marriage" advises husband and wife to take these prayers to heart and soul.

Mutual Respect and Appreciation

Spouses must respect one another at all times.

Queen Vashti, the wife of King Xerxes in Shushan, disrespected her husband by refusing to attend to his call when he sent for her in the presence of dignitaries. He deposed her and replaced her with Queen Esther who eventually used her position to deliver the Jews who were to be annihilated. Vashti's disrespect and disobedience brought her down from grace to grass.

Queen Vashti has done wrong, not only against the king but also against all the nobles and the peoples of all the provinces of King Xerxes. For the queen's conduct will become known to all the women, and so they will despise their husbands and say, 'King Xerxes commanded Queen Vashti to be brought before him, but she would not come.' This very day the Persian and Medean women of the nobility who have heard about the Queen's conduct will respond to all the King's nobles in the same way. There will be no end of disrespect and discord. Therefore, if it pleases the King, let him issue a royal decree and let it be written in the laws of Persia and Medea, which cannot be repealed, that Vashti is never again to enter the presence of King Xerxes. Also let the King give her royal position to someone else who is better than she. (Esther 1: 16-19)

Allow me to use my own marriage as an example of how mutual respect can keep a marriage strong.

There are many ways I show my husband respect both at home and at work, even as we operate our family business in the same office. When my children needed anything when they were growing up, I would always ask my husband for his permission despite the fact that I had full access to all our resources. He always gave his approval, always wondering why I ever needed to ask him first. To me it is a sign of the mutual respect the "University of Marriage" teaches.

When I give an assignment to our office staff and my husband gives the same person another assignment, I mandate my staff to execute his errand before mine. Our staff say that they have learnt a lot from our union and relationship. In likewise manner, a colleague at the bank where I worked twenty-five years ago noticed a behaviour that pleasantly surprised him. There were no mobile phones at the time, and three or four desks shared one external telephone line. A person's call could come through on somebody else's desk. My colleague noticed that anytime my husband called, no matter on which desk the call arrived, I would drop anything and everything to attend to him quickly. He applauded and admired my behaviour. To me this was and is second nature, for my husband deserves to be tended to immediately.

My husband returns the gesture. While staff tend to give more attention and respect to men, my husband won't allow this in our house. I have observed on many occasions that my husband corrects any new chauffeur who rushes past me to open the car door for my husband first. My husband always sends the chauffeur back to tend to me first.

A simple lesson at the "University of Marriage" is that appreciating your spouse encourages the spouse to appreciate you. While these are but small examples of mutual respect and appreciation, it is through these small things that the day-to-day life of a long marriage can not only be successful, but pleasant as well.

If you do not know, O fairest among women, follow in the footsteps of the flock, and feed your little goats beside the shepherds' tents. I have compared you, my love, to my filly among Pharaoh's chariots. Your cheeks are lovely with ornaments, your neck with chains of gold. (Solo 1:8-10)

Mutual Tolerance, Patience, Encouragement and Empathy

Husbands and wives must be tolerant and patient towards one another. Even if one spouse has bad habits, the other should pray for him or her. Stormie Omartian once urged women to pray: "Lord, give my husband a new wife, but let it be me." This means, no matter how intolerable or difficult her husband may be, God should give her the grace to be patient enough to accommodate and accept him for who he is. Also, his love for her should be renewed constantly, as though they were newly married.

The flipside of this coin is the need for spouses to encourage one another in every way, most especially when one is going through a difficult period in his or her life.

Two are better than one, because they have a good reward for their labour. For if they fall, one will lift up his companion. But woe to him who is alone when he falls.
(Eccl. 4:9-10)

When my mother died at the age of 92, I had my husband's shoulder to cry on. His comfort and advice were invaluable and his words of encouragement soothing. His empathy for my situation made my lot much more bearable.

Support and encouragement is most dearly needed if your spouse is going down a road you are not comfortable with. For as God has endowed each one of us with special gifts for various purposes, we may not always understand the road our partner wishes to take. Each spouse should find out and cherish their divine gifts, and support each other in using and developing them.

For in fact the body is not one member but many. If the foot should say, "Because I am not a hand, I am not of the body," is it therefore not of the body? And if the ear should say, "Because I am not an eye, I am not of the body," " is it therefore not of the body? (1 Cor 12:14-17)

Communication

A marriage cannot blossom without open and honest communication between husband and wife, and no communication will be open, honest *and* successful without a healthy dose of humour. For spouses should be able to look forward to and enjoy each other's company.

A merry heart does good, like medicine, but a broken spirit dries the bones. (Prov. 17:22)

Humour can bridge gaps, tackle problems, heal wounds and open the lines of communication between husband and wife. Humour is vital, because it is important that husband and wife have a good rapport through both verbal and body language. Remember never to forget even the smallest detail, as the right word at the right time might make the difference in any relationship.

Anxiety in the heart of man causes depression, but a good word makes it glad. (Prov. 12:25)

Spousal communication should be encouraging, honest, respectful and kind.

Let no corrupt word proceed out of your mouth, but what is good for necessary edification, that it may impart grace to the hearers. (Eph 4:29)

In other words, communication between spouses should adhere by the rules established for any conduct between the married couple, and show mutual respect and appreciation, tolerance and patience, encouragement and empathy – for it is then that the unity has a chance to survive, even if it has to weather many storms.

The Gift of Time

Everything needs time and care; a relationship is no exception. Spouses should choose their jobs carefully, so that they can spend time with their family. Every member of the family needs each other, as all have a vital role to play.

It is better to avoid bringing work home and to ensure that your spouse is not left alone too often. You must not be too busy to attend to your spouse's needs and desires, or your spouse may look elsewhere for their desired needs. Both spouses must learn to plan their days, weeks and months to allot enough time for work and wife, home and husband. Both spouses must also make enough time to tend their health and beauty so as to remain attractive to each other.

In other words, spouses must make time for each other, and as parents they must make time for their children. Family life must be a value unto its own, for if it takes a backseat to a career or individual enjoyment, the marriage will go astray.

No career and no amount of money that may sit in your bank account; no mansion you may live in; no piece of furniture that may grace your living room; no piece of art that hangs on your wall will ever matter as much as the love you have for your family. Our treasures on Earth are not supposed to be more important than those waiting for us in Heaven based on our purpose and achievements here.

Do not lay up for yourselves treasures on earth, where moth and rust destroy and where thieves break in and steal; but lay up for yourselves treasures in heaven, where neither moth nor rust destroys and where thieves do not break in and steal. (Matt 6:19-20)

Therefore one of the most important lessons the "University of Marriage" can teach you is to try not to be overwhelmed by the demands of your daily life, but instead to acknowledge the blessing that is your family. Spend a few quiet moments with your spouse at the end of a busy day; share a meal with your children; spend time together as a family over the weekends; celebrate birthdays and anniversaries; revel in your children's achievements whether big or small; and do so every day. For God's light upon you shines never brighter than when He blesses you with a happy family life.

PART II

Common Reasons Why Marriages Fail

1. Infidelity and Promiscuity

Infidelity seems to be a common ill in modern marriages. There are many reasons for this development. Female emancipation, which has brought supposed equality to men and women, has made financial independence an attainable goal for women and therefore many have lost interest in marriage. Consequently they may change partners frequently and be promiscuous before they settle down, if they ever do. Women who are married and work at the same time are too busy to be bothered with mastering the art of building a home, which may lead their husbands to look elsewhere for proper "marital" care and attention.

Men, on the other hand, are quite attracted to (financially) independent women and some even think it is cheaper, safer and sometimes even lucrative to go after a married woman depending on how affluent she is. All too often this leads to the adulterous behaviour of a wife. Many married men feel overworked and underpaid and complain that their wives are preoccupied with their children and they want to let off steam and stress in the arms of other women. All too often this leads to adulterous behaviour of a husband, which is not a surprise given that men are outnumbered and surrounded by women who flaunt themselves.

While all of the above may be an explanation for these recent developments, none of it is an excuse for the chaos, infidelity, cheating, lying, secret candle-lit dinners and weekend getaways of illicit love affairs.

In the olden days, male promiscuity was common, and African women were quite content to share their husbands, living in communal settings where everyone understood the rules. Wives knew to take turns in living with their husband on a regular rotational basis. A wife would move in with her bed linen and cooking utensils to replace the wife before her, only to be replaced by the next when her turn was over. This arrangement seemed to ensure that the man did not have the urge to seek further attention outside his own home. The wives either co-operated well amongst one another or were bitter enemies who quarrelled constantly, depending on how their husband handled his family. Some men would instil discipline amongst their wives while others would let them carry on, proud that women were fighting over them.

At the time, women believed that it was essential to stay put and not leave their husbands for the sake of their children's future, no matter how difficult their marital life might have been. Of course it helped that even if they tried to return to their parents, they would be chased back. Marriage in Africa has always been seen as a union of the two families first, and a union of the couple second. Therefore, a wife had nowhere to go when she tried to leave her husband. As a result, there were not many divorces in those days. It was a man's world, and women hardly had any opportunities to make their own choices.

In the Western world, in Europe or the USA, the situation was not much different. Women were not 'handed over' to their husband's family to stick it out no matter what, but they were stay-at-home housewives whose destiny was to cook and clean and look after their husbands and children. Even Western women stayed in unhappy marriages for their children's welfare and out of fear of the shame a divorce would bring.

Times have changed both in Africa and in the West. Many husbands and wives don't see eye to eye anymore. Some have married the wrong partner for the wrong reasons, be that a desire for financial stability or social status; some have accepted the first partner who would have them even though they were not compatible; others have married out of infatuation or for lust; yet others have married just to leave behind lonely single lives. Years later they realize that the decision to marry this partner, or even that to marry at all, was wrong. While in the olden days nothing would change and the marital union would stay intact, these days men and women tend to act upon their realisation and more often than not this leads to broken homes.

The case of a young couple I recently met illustrates this point.

Husband and wife could not be more different: she is an extrovert and he, an introvert. The wife married him because her biological clock was ticking and all her friends were already married. However, soon neither was deriving any pleasure from the relationship and they were both unhappy. She felt he was too quiet and boring, and he felt she didn't appreciate him enough. Things were falling apart because his eye had wandered and one thing led to another. The marriage was at an end due to the husband's infidelity.

Another young couple had married out of love, yet infidelity broke their marriage.

At first the marriage seemed to work just fine. The husband hardly left home except to go to work. However, when work carried him to another part of the country, he started dating another woman there. One day his wife paid a visit without prior notice and found out about the affair. She confronted him, but he offered no explanation or apology. Desperate to be loved, his wife engaged in affairs of her own. When her husband found out, they separated, although his wife had repented, cried and pined. Their marriage failed due to the adultery of both spouses.

Here's another story that illustrates my point about adultery:

Many years ago, a beautiful young lady with a domineering spirit went after a young doctor who was managing his father's hospital and was already married. Although the marriage was having problems, he did not divorce his wife. This lady used to visit him in the hospital and they ended up having a son, obviously in sin. Unfortunately, they later discovered the boy had hearing problems; he was diagnosed and treated from country to country to no avail. While the woman was still struggling with that, she and I became close.

She saw me as a role model and liked to copy a lot of things I did; like the kind of car I drove, where I shopped, and the kind of clothes and shoes I wore. Slowly I began to notice that she would come to our home in the evenings after office hours on days when she was wearing a new outfit, though we worked in the same establishment. She enjoyed the compliments my husband and I gave her. I also began to notice that she would change her step and looks whenever my husband was around. Yet when my husband was not around she never stayed long. In short, all she said and did pointed to the fact that she was aiming for my husband's favour right under my nose. I immediately drew my husband's attention to her hidden agenda and we both decided to start giving her the cold shoulder. She got the message and that was how I was able to get rid of her.

I was observant and the bond to my husband was healthy and strong enough to withstand danger from the outside in the shape of a woman with insincere intentions. Another woman, who is much older than me, was not so lucky.

She came across a middle aged lady on board an international flight and took to her immediately because she looked so much like her daughter. They became family friends despite the age disparity and before you could say Jack Robinson, she was pregnant with madam's husband's baby. When she had the baby, God ensured the boy did not look anything like the young lady's husband but was the spitting image of the sugar daddy. Before long, the young couple moved house to a highbrow neighbourhood and they suddenly began to live in affluence, profiting from her sin. When friends confronted her husband with the rumour going around, he refuted it because he was enjoying the new lease of life, though he knew the truth in his heart. However, the marriage eventually broke up when the money finished and she moved out to the United States of America to start a new life. She has now repented and become a Pastor while her husband is still depressed and battling with life on his own. ∎

Whilst it is not a crime to meet someone and take an immediate liking to the person, we must ask God about them before they start getting too close to us and our family so that we do not make wrong choices. After all, God has given us the power to choose. We must learn not to be too trusting of mankind and instead make "In God We Trust" the philosophy that guides our lives.

The senior sister of a friend of mine has had quite a rough marital life because she trusted a "stranger". She had been working in the visa section of an embassy abroad and helped someone who had some difficulty with his application for an extended visa. He wormed his way into her heart and before long; they got married and had two children. He had financial difficulties with completing his education, so she carried on working to pay his way through university. He then relocated ahead to his homeland, Nigeria, "to prepare the way" for his family, or so he claimed.

Her deceiving husband built a house and moved another woman into it while he kept his real wife abroad. When the news filtered to her in Europe, she changed jobs to be in her homeland, and accommodation was provided for her in a highbrow area. Her husband quickly moved in with her, leaving the other woman in his house but always scrambled out on Sundays to take his second wife to church, leaving his first wife at home. Of course, for how long could any relationship like this last? Things fell apart; his wife left her lucrative oil company job and shipped out to the USA with her sons for university degrees. The husband moved back to the house he built and to his new found "wife". He had finished using his first wife for his education and is now living with another woman in the house built from his wife's sweat. The irony of life. ■

It is essential to learn from other people's mistakes and ask for divine wisdom because there are just too many spouse-snatchers about (Prov. 7:1-5). This man was a liar, a cheat, and a heartless advantage-seeker who used her for his own gain.

Nevertheless, a wife or husband, whether divorced or not, must forgive their spouse so that God can continue to answer their prayers.

For if you forgive men their trespasses, your heavenly Father will also forgive you. But if you do not forgive men their trespasses, neither will your Father forgive your trespasses.
(Matt 6:14-15)

Women can wrong their men as badly as men wrong their women. Take the case of the Christian couple below.

The husband had a good job, was gentle, and quiet, homely by nature, and he loved his wife dearly. When he lost his job, his wife claimed she did not love him anymore. Apparently, she had been having affairs with other men despite the fact that they had a lovely home and well behaved children. She decided to leave him although her friends pleaded with her and her husband assured her of his love. She was more interested in another woman's husband, who apparently was a 'Romeo' busy painting the town red. This marriage ended due to her promiscuity, and now her children must grow up without their mother.

My, son, keep my words and treasure my commands within you. Keep my commands and live, and my law as the apple of your eye. Bind them on your fingers; write them on the tablet of your heart. Say to wisdom, "You are my sister, "and call understanding your nearest kin, that they may keep you from the immoral woman from the seductress who flatters with her words. (Prov 7:1-5)

The "University of Marriage" teaches that men need to run away from seductive women who will stop at nothing to get their way.

Do not lust after her beauty in your heart, nor let her allure you with her eyelids. For by means of a harlot, a man is reduced to a crust of bread; and an adulteress will prey upon his precious life. (Prov 6:25-26)

A marriage can only survive if both husband and wife are committed to the union and do their very best not to walk astray by committing adultery. However, men are more prone to unfaithfulness and promiscuity than women, who are usually quite content looking after their spouse, children and the household. In fact, many may be too preoccupied with their role and responsibility for so many people that there is hardly enough time for "extracurricular" activities.

Upon finding out about their husbands' promiscuity, some

wives get so frustrated that they overreact.

One woman I know cut up all her husband's ties and ruined his suits upon learning that her husband had betrayed her. She then moved back to her parents' house but they sent her back to resolve the problems with her husband. Before she returned, her husband had become born again. Realising what he had done, he apologised to his wife and took her back. They now go to church together and he has become an evangelist.

Bursts of anger cannot help the situation; of course, the only thing that helps is if both husband and wife re-commit to the sacred union of their marriage.

Another lady poured hot water on her husband because he was always cheating, lying, abusing her person and degrading her.

Being constantly on our knees in prayer for our loved ones is important and much more successful than being on our feet to fight, for it is our conduct that can make our spouses change positively.

Arise, cry out in the night, at the beginning of the watches; pour out your heart like water before the face of the Lord. Lift your hands toward Him for the life of your young children, who faint from hunger at the head of every street.
(Lamentations 2:19)

It is a hard lesson to learn at the "University of Marriage" that instead of showing anger or frustration, a scorned woman must pray for her loved one as much as a scorned man, for we need to

break any yoke of bondage that may be hanging over our spouses
Learn to say arrow prayers (quick prayers under your breath),
which, if prayed from the heart, effect instant and miraculous
change in the person's words and attitude.

The blood of Jesus prevails over you.

I rebuke you foul spirit in the name of Jesus.

I bind and cast you out now in the name of Jesus.

Father, let this storm be still NOW in Jesus name.

It is only our loving conduct that can affect a positive change
in our marital union, which despite all personal heartache, is and
remains a wife and a husband's God-given destiny.

2. Interference by In-Laws

There is hardly a marriage where in-laws do not interfere unless the husband puts an end to it. If in-laws interfere it is usually the husband's choice, as the wife is the one who will be engaged in a running battle to fend them off. Most wives want their in-laws outlawed!

Most in-law problems are between mother-in-law and daughter-in-law, with the husband or son caught in-between. Often the husband is too weak to know how to handle the situation, too indecisive to know whose side to take, or too self-involved to end the battle because he feels it is enjoyable to watch two women fight over him, even if they are from two different generations.

More often than not, the mother-in-law wants to control her son's wife and take over the running of her home. Many mothers-in-law criticise everything her daughter-in-law does or doesn't do.

The mother-in-law might criticise the daughter-in-law's cooking, her children and the way she raises them, the way she interacts, treats or relates to her husband and even the way she dresses. Some mothers-in-law cannot stand the idea that another woman has taken their place and has more of their sons' attention. To many mothers-in-law, the son's wife is competition that needs to be tackled.

Obviously, this puts the husband in a difficult position given that this is a tug of war between the two women he loves the most in the world.

Sometimes even a sister-in-law causes problems in her brother's marriage. Most of the time, the reason for interference by a sister-in-law is petty jealousy. Many also feel that the new woman, the wife, has stolen their breadwinner and they are prepared to do anything to 'get him back'.

Many in-laws can be mean and unrelenting in their interference, even to the point of frustrating the new wife so much that she sees no way out other than leaving her husband. An example of this behaviour is in the following story:

After her husband lost his job, the wife was providing for the home. Her husband's brothers would come and stay with them at her expense. She would shop and cook for them, even after a long day at work. The husband's brothers always served themselves first, and sometimes the children would go hungry. Once in a while the brothers offered to wash clothes of everyone in the household except those of the wife. She provided money for their maintenance, even including medical treatment. The wife was so frustrated that before too long she resolved to leave and stay with her parents until her husband and his brothers resolve the issues at hand. ■

Hostility from in-laws can even start in the period of courtship, when the son brings home his fiancée to introduce her to the family. If his parents and siblings don't really like her immediately, trouble most likely lies ahead.

One vital lesson the "University of Marriage" teaches is that to avoid unpleasant face-offs, it is wise to think ahead and determine ways to put things in a positive perspective. Both future couples as well as future in-laws need to play their part in welcoming each other into their lives. If the new couple has reason to believe that the in-laws may feel left out of the marriage arrangements, they should make sure they have adequate say in all the arrangements. Also, the in-laws should accept their son or daughter's choice and be glad to gain a son or daughter rather than fear they will lose one.

In-laws should leave the new couple alone to begin their life journey in peace, even if they would have preferred to do things differently. After all, they have had their chance to make their choices and build a life. Now it is time to allow the young couple to build theirs. This is not such a difficult task - all it takes is that all parties show a little kindness, which costs so little but achieves so much.

Things are a bit more difficult if in-laws must live with the couple, for then two ways of life have to be merged together. If in any way possible, in-laws should have their separate apartments and kitchens, so the young couple can be given as much privacy as possible. However, in order to cement a good relationship, the young couple should try to learn a few things from the in-laws, especially live-in mothers-in-law. Young couples should remember that the older generation do know a few things that are worth listening to. By the same token, change is good, and the younger generation should be free to try things out. In short, both, parents-in-law and the new couple should do the very best to accommodate each other and to learn from each other. With prayer, patience, wisdom and a good attitude towards one another, peace will reign.

Sometimes even widows are not even left alone by their in-laws. In fact, there may be accusations that make a widow even more miserable during and/or after mourning the death of the husband.

Sometimes widows are accused of having killed their husbands and the in-laws are ready to go to any lengths to prove it and/or avenge the death of their son/brother.

Bomi was recently introduced to The Rose of Sharon Foundation, a foundation for widows and orphans, shortly after she narrowly escaped being lynched by her in-laws. Bomi and her husband had built a new home in a remote area, and when armed robbers came knocking, her husband locked his family in the kitchen and went out to combat the robbers. The robbers shot him, yet her in-laws accused his widow of foul play. One day, as she was driving out with her family and their Reverend, her in-laws arrived and threatened to pour petrol all over the car and set them ablaze in retaliation for having 'killed their bread-winner'. They eventually relented on the Reverend's insistence that if they killed her, they would have to kill him, too. She quickly packed, left the house and ran for dear life with her children. Although she had an MBA and

was a former bank employee, her husband had forced her to
resign her position to look after their six children, which left
her scrambling for survival after her husband's death.

Why would any woman want to kill the goose that laid the
golden egg? But all too often, any excuse will do for in-laws to
kick out the widow and take over the dead man's property.

3. Substance Abuse

There is no doubt that some marriages are plagued with bad habits. Sometimes these habits are a result of marital problems, and sometimes they are hereditary traits that were not obvious during courtship. What does the "University of Marriage" suggest should be done in such cases? Are we supposed to stay in abusive relationships for the sake of keeping up the holy union of matrimony? In the olden days, the answer would have been a resounding 'yes'. Now each situation must be reviewed on an individual basis.

Consider the case of Nneka. Her marriage was challenging and traumatic. A single mother had raised Nneka, and had done her best to keep the girl away from men, and did not even explain what to expect from men or how to behave in any kind of relationship, completely shielding her children from outsiders except when in school. So, Nneka had an absentee father, and a mother who did not impart values and information. It was not until she got to university that she made a few friends. She became a lawyer and met her husband-to-be, also a lawyer. They were married six months later, because she became pregnant, he wanted the child and promised to provide for his family. All seemed well, but unfortunately, he changed after the wedding and started treating her like a maid. He would shout at her, constantly going over the apartment with "a magnifying glass", nit-picking and if he found any dust on his finger, it would land on her cheek. In front of her children, he would demand that she kneel down and beg his forgiveness anytime he was upset with her. Soon she feared him and froze in terror at the sound of his footsteps. She dreaded being around him.

Her husband had been earning a paltry salary and she had not yet found a job, which forced her to manage on the little house keeping allowance he gave her. She did, but he complained nonetheless, claiming that the amount of beef or fish in his meals was too small. When he lost his job due to his behaviour at work a few days after their second child was born, she had to go out in search of work. Through the assistance of relatives she got a job, which, from the description in the employment letter, seemed perfect. He demanded her salary, and when she initially refused because she needed it to take care of the household, he got violently angry.

One day when she needed money to pay a workman for an emergency repair, she looked through his pockets to find the necessary cash, but instead she found marijuana! His substance abuse explained his terrible mood swings, and so she confronted him. Yet instead of being apologetic, he was recalcitrant and blamed her.

Nneka was too depressed to do anything about her situation, as she wondered what people would say if she left him and became a single parent. She also did not want to repeat her mother's hard life as a single parent. She knew very little about Jesus and the power of His resurrection that would have given her strength and deliverance, so she just accepted her situation as it was, and decided to be submissive and obedient rather than confrontational.

Life went on. She put in her best at work, knowing full well that they needed the income. All this brought about petty jealousy in him. Anytime she came home with anything new for the children or herself, he would rant and rave out of jealousy. He made constant sexual demands on her out of excessive desire, not in honour.

...each of you should know how to possess his own vessel in sanctification and honour, not in passion of lust, like the Gentiles who do not know God. (1 Thessalonians 4:4-5)

One day things went out of hand he started banging her head against the wall. When he finally let go of her, he went to the two children, laid his hands on their heads and rained curses on them. She cancelled all the curses as he was blurting them out and at that point, the camel's back broke. She called her uncles who came to get her immediately. Their marriage was beyond repair and they split up.

If we analyse her situation, we realise that her troubles began even before the marriage, as she was naïve in her choice of husband. She went into the marriage without knowledge of the lessons the "University of Marriage" teaches. This is due to the fact that her mother did not allow any interaction with others during her teenage years, and, as a single mother, could not impart any knowledge of the challenges of courtship and married life. Furthermore, their courtship was rather short, allowing little room to get to know her man well. In other words, she did not look before she leapt, and did not even check her husband's background. Having sex before marriage got her pregnant, and thus she married not only the wrong man, but also for the wrong reason. She did not marry out of true love, but out of necessity. Once they were married, she bottled everything up and just kept accepting her husband's behaviour without trying to communicate with him. Finally, she was not a deep Christian who knew how to consult with the Lord for guidance.

Her situation clearly was bad, and beyond repair towards the end. Yet there are some things she could and should have done in their relationship. The confrontational rather than communicative and supportive tone of her home could have been steered in the right direction had she followed God's command. God requires total submission of the wife to the husband, and this includes submission of everything you own and all you are. Therefore she should not have refused to hand over her salary, she should not have refused to register her car in his name, nor should she have refused to submit to his physical needs as he demanded. Perhaps he would have been able to do without drugs if their marriage had been happier.

Therefore, just as the church is subject to Christ, so let the wives be to their own husbands in everything. (Ephesians 5:24)

If her conduct alone did not help the situation, she should have requested spiritual support in her local church. Christian brothers and sisters would have helped her deal with the evil spirit of substance abuse, which needed to be cast out of her home. Had she, in time, applied God's command, He would have come to her aid.

Finally, be strong in the Lord and in his mighty power. Put on the full armour of God, so that you can take your stand against the devil's schemes. For our struggle is not against flesh and blood, but against the rulers, against the authorities, against the powers of this dark world and against the spiritual forces of evil in the heavenly realms. Therefore put on the full armour of God, so that when the day of evil comes, you may be able to stand your ground, and after you have done everything, to stand. Stand firm then, with the belt of truth buckled around your waist, with the breastplate of righteousness in place, and with your feet fitted with the readiness that comes from the gospel of peace. In addition to all this, take up the shield of faith, with which you can extinguish all the flaming arrows of the evil one. Take the helmet of salvation and the sword of the Spirit, which is the word of God. And pray in the Spirit on all occasions with all kinds of prayers and requests. With this in mind, be alert and always keep on praying for all the Lord's people. (Eph 6:10-18)

In addition, she should have instituted a family worship, even if he did not fulfil his duty as spiritual leader of the household. No prayer ever goes to waste, and her spiritual guidance might have turned him and her family around. For as the "University of Marriage" teaches, our loving conduct can improve a difficult marital situation.

4. Withholding Physical Affection

When two people get married, they become one flesh.

Therefore a man shall leave his father and mother and be joined to his wife, and they shall become one flesh. (Gen. 2:24)

Husband and wife have to feel love and affection for one another. Each is the one who has more authority over the body of the partner.

Let the husband render to his wife the affection due her, and likewise also the wife to her husband. The wife does not have authority over her own body, but the husband does. And likewise the husband does not have authority over his own body, but the wife does. Do not deprive one another except with consent for a time that you may give yourselves to fasting and prayer; and come together again so that Satan

does not tempt you because of your lack of self-control.
(1 Cor. 7:3-5)

However, using physical affection, or rather, withholding physical affection as punishment is an unholy act and not the will of God. The Bible tells us that the only time we should not make ourselves (our bodies, our temples) available to our partners is when we are fasting. Even then, permission must be sought from the partner before embarking on a fasting period.

Unfortunately many modern couples no longer abide by this simple rule, and often husbands and wives find reason not to grant power over their bodies to their spouse. Wives may go on strike when their husbands do not honour their financial responsibility to their families. Husbands may ignore their wives when engrossed with other women. Unfortunately, no one ever seems to think of the consequences of such actions. When physical affection is withheld, the spouse might look for pleasure elsewhere, or else might feel unloved and begin to suspect that the spouse is unfaithful; some might even react negatively, keep malice or get violent.

It is plainly obvious that this behaviour does not help any relationship but rather drives a wedge between husband and wife. Vindictive justice will breed animosity. Rather than get back at each other by withholding physical affection, you should try and get back together by making yourself available for one another.

Many modern couples have separate bedrooms. Whilst there may seem to be nothing wrong with that, it also does not help a relationship. Couples can be so far from each other when they own separate bedrooms that making up after quarrels (which are bound to happen) becomes difficult. If on the other hand, they share the same bed, avoiding one another in the same bedroom is near impossible and making up becomes almost a matter of course. For the same reason, Queen size beds are preferable over King size beds, because in a bed that is too big, spouses tend to move away from one another rather than closer. Given that physical closeness is the goal and means of any successful marriage, the arrangement and look of the couple's bedroom is so much more than interior decoration. All husbands and wives should make sure that their bedrooms, as well as their behaviour within, is conducive to spousal relations.

Common Reasons Why Marriages Fail

5. Financial Issues

Finances are a crucial tool for every marriage. Sufficient finances cushion, comfort and help sustain a marriage, but only if well managed. If financial security turns into a bedrock and takes the place of love, or if lack of finances bring strife, anger, failure, frustration and even temptation to seek safety elsewhere, worldly possessions become a bone of contention in a relationship that is supposed to be made in Heaven. In such a case it is, as the "University of Marriage" teaches us all along, time to go back to basics.

The Bible teaches us to be content with what we have.

Let your conduct be without covetousness; be content with such things as you have. (Heb 13:5a)

Therefore, even if a couple are not well off, if they are content with what they have, it should not cause problems between them.

Now godliness with contentment is great gain. (1 Tim 6:6)

Clearly there are issues that complicate the situation. If one spouse has more money than the other and hides or hoards it, not allowing the other spouse access to the funds, serious marital problems ensue. Worse still, if a spouse purchases land, real estate, stock and shares secretly, the marriage is not a true partnership and therefore bound to run into trouble. When the wife conducts financial business this way, more often than not it is due to a perceived need to provide enough house-keeping allowance for her family, either because the husband is not able to, or because he chooses not to do so because he spends his money elsewhere, on girlfriends and/or his extended family or other people and things. When the husband conducts financial business this way, more often than not it is due to his desire as the head of the household to be in charge and take control.

Such behaviour does not take into account one of the simple lessons of the "University of Marriage": God demands that couples share everything they have and not use it as a weapon against the other.

Consider this example:

A brother called Tunde once said that his wife was always very stubborn, rude, and too lazy to do housework. He punished her by giving her little or no house keeping allowance. As a consequence, she was even less inclined to fulfil her God-given duty as a homebuilder, and accusations and counter-accusations ensued. However, the couple have been counselled several times and things have begun to improve. She has been encouraged to improve on her attitude, to be polite, patient, and respectful. She is to desist from talking back and to look after the home rather than playing the tit-for-tat game. She was also told to be prudent and diligent and was referred to God's will in the Bible. The counselling given to both spouses has turned their relationship around. Her husband recently financed a holiday abroad for her and their son and all is well. ■

A prudent woman is cautious and possesses good judgment and discretion. Just like Abigail, the wife of Nabal (the wealthy man who refused to help by feeding David and his men), who discreetly changed David's anger into admiration.

A good wife works hard to ensure she has enough food at home for her family. Clothing and clean comfortable surroundings to make her family happy are paramount on her mind. She must be a model of efficiency in order to be able to increase her family's resources through her wise investment and productive management of all in her care.

She also rises while it is yet night, and provides food for her household, and a portion for her maidservants. She considers a field and buys it; from her profits she plants a vineyard. She girds herself with strength, and strengthens her arms. She perceives that her merchandise is good, and her lamp does not go out by night.(Prov 31:15-18)

A good wife would know that a woman who does not submit to or respect her man could never find favour in God's sight.

Lolade – although a good wife, not temperamental, apologetic, patient, respectful and submissive – did not quite know the extent of submission required of women by God. As a woman, do all that the Bible says in (Eph. 5:22-24), "stand!" By "stand" I mean wait and see how God will fight for you. God watches every move, sees every heart and punishes all disobedience even after repentance and forgiveness. Maybe Lolade's husband would have been a changed man had she submitted to him completely, and the marriage might have been saved. ■

A good husband, on the other hand, is to provide for his wife and children and must do so in obedience to God, regardless of whether he is happy with his wife or not. He is not to be the judge of his wife; he is to leave that to God.

Judge not, that you be not judged. (Matthew 7:1)

A good husband does not use money to punish his wife for her insubordination as this can frustrate a woman so much and push her to take desperate measures.

Vengeance is Mine, and recompense; their foot shall slip in due time; for the day of their calamity is at hand, and the things to come hasten upon them. (Deut. 32:35)

Husbands must fulfil their role as provider. If he falls short even though he tries his best, he has to take it to the Lord in prayer, to Him who promised He would never leave us nor forsake us.

For He Himself has said, "I will never leave you nor forsake you." (Heb 13:5b)

Part of the husband's role as provider is to make sure they live within their means. Clearly, some men are more concerned about themselves than about the welfare of their families, spending money on other women, their hobbies, their friends, their personal desires and in some cases, even drugs before they tend to their family's needs. Make no mistake: God judges such men.

See how God judged Kola as you read further:

Ann and Kola had courted for almost two years. She had a very good job with a bank, while he was an artist who lived in Ghana. They finally got married and he tried to persuade her to leave her job behind and move with him back to Ghana. Luckily for her she asked for advice and her colleagues insisted that she keep her job, though at a lower pay and position since the bank did not need staff at her level outside Lagos. She had acquired a lot of furniture, which they sent ahead with her other belongings, and the office offered her accommodation in Ghana. On their way to Ghana, her husband disappeared for several hours at one of the stops only to emerge looking 'wild' without any explanation. When they got to their new home, strangers staying in the house and wearing her clothes met them. When she asked who they were, her husband told her to shut up as they were his friends. These so-called friends stayed, using her furniture, and eating her food, smoked and took drugs to the point that she locked herself in her room and cried every day. Her only safe and sane moments were at work, for she felt like a frightened stranger in her own home. Things came to a head when he kicked down her door and reigned abuses on her. She subsequently suffered a stroke from the abuse, and she had nowhere to go, because she was new in Ghana and hadn't made any friends. And even if she had left, she was afraid he would find her.

In her despair, she, who was not used to praying before, began to pray to God from her heart. Of course, God answers prayers. Before long, her husband had a run-in with the law and was traced to the house where he made a quick getaway. He never returned. She was then able to report her case to the police, she changed accommodation and door locks. She went into therapy and treatment for her stroke in the USA after which she was able to return to her normal life. Her face however remains slightly disfigured. ■

Vengeance is Mine, and recompense;

Their foot shall slip in due time;

For the day of their calamity is at hand,

And the things to come hasten upon them. (Deuteronomy 32:35)

There are other clear cases of men who put their desires and pleasures before their family. Read on:

A friend once told me that her husband was more interested in his polo horses than his wife and children. He did not mind spending any amount of money on his horses while his children led a second-class lifestyle. She had to threaten to leave him before he even began to look their way. ■

Common Reasons Why Marriages Fail

6. Class Issues

It is best to marry in the right social class in a society or community. The right class of course is the class similar to the one you belong to. Moving into a different class instead may cause chaos and trouble within both, your nuclear and the extended families. Class differences create an inferiority/superiority complex, which all too easily breeds jealousy.

Consider this example:

Karen and Jide got married about seven years ago despite heavy protests from the bride's parents. Her family was quite wealthy, and her parents felt that their daughter was too good for the groom although he was a university graduate, because his family was poor. Karen had studied in England and had just returned to Nigeria when she met Jide and they fell in love, despite their differences in background and upbringing. Jide lived in a run-down area of town, but when they married, Karen didn't care about her new dilapidated surroundings, because she was madly in love.

Unfortunately, although educated at university, Jide could not find a job. Before long, he started to abuse and "tongue-lash" her, calling her a spoilt brat. He kept her from mingling with her "high-class" friends, as he called them, and kept her grounded at home as if to punish her for his misfortune of coming from a less-privileged family. He seemed to take his frustration out on her more and more, and even began beating her at will. At first, Karen was too ashamed to tell her parents what was going on, but eventually she packed her belongings and left, never to return.

This example is not meant to show that people of two different social classes cannot have a successful relationship. In the end, social class is meaningless for Christians. What this story shows is that if a couple is not well matched, differences in background and upbringing may become the bone of contention that ruins the relationship. If a couple does not have enough common ground to build upon, a marriage is doomed to failure. Therefore it is vital to talk to God before we make any important decisions. Had Karen prayed for advice before she chose her mate, she likely would not have gotten married to Jide and heartache could have been avoided.

7. Lack of Open and Respectful Communication

Many couples carry on living together with very little or sometimes no communication for days, months or even years. They get comfortable keeping malice with one another, harbouring ill feelings that fester and grow. However, God demands that we resolve our differences, and do so as soon as possible.

"Be angry, and do not sin," and do not let the sun go down on your wrath. (Eph 4:26)

God's demand is wise because it ensures that quarrels do not escalate or degenerate. We must not leave room for Satan to put a wedge between us and our fellow human beings, most definitely not in marital relationships. Consider this example from my own marital life:

I remember once when my husband was very upset with me and I did not want to argue although I felt he had gone overboard with his anger at the time. I swallowed my pride and to his surprise, I begged him, cuddled and comforted him. That night the Lord opened my eyes in a dream. He showed me evil spirits that were looking down into our bedroom, who were rather baffled that I was not angry but did what I could to end our marital spat. I heard them say to one another that the others should come closer to see what was going on in our house. "They are already talking to one another!" God had opened the lower heaven for me to know that my actions had been a small victory over Satan's kingdom.

Humility, communication, interaction, perseverance and patience helped me then. Had I instead held a grudge and not made up and communicated with my husband that night, Satan's ways would have won a victory instead. Consider this example:

A sister once told me that her husband enjoys keeping malice and that although she tried not to follow suit during the early years of their marriage, now, after more than eighteen years, a competition has ensued between them to see who could outlast the other before talking to the other. Such a couple is keeping Satan and his kingdom very happy, for when a marriage is plagued with an atmosphere of animosity, anger, strife and arrogance, one thing will lead to the other, the relationship will deteriorate even more and may lead to separation or even divorce. By that time of course, the deed is done and the relationship is difficult or impossible to mend except by the sheer grace of God.

Here is another example of the dangers of lack of communication:

> It is the story of a brother who is fond of boasting that his wife does not know anything about him or anything he is planning, and shows the dangers of a lack of communication. This husband believes that wives should never be part of a decision making process, but if at all, should only be told later. However, such an attitude only helps to relegate his wife to the background and creates a distance between the couple. ■

A wife should always be treated with respect, like a partner rather than an employee. Plans and decisions should be made together because each partner has a God-given role to play within the marriage.

Of course, not all communication is successful. An argumentative and nagging tone in marital communication can be as damaging as no communication at all. It is not uncommon for a newly wed couple to get on each other's nerves shortly after the marriage ceremony. The fanfare is over and the relatives and guests have gone home. All too often arguments ensue as the couple begins to settle into a new life together, discovering behavioural or character traits about each other that may not go down well. A very typical example is the matter of neatness: some spouses must have everything around them squeaky clean while the other is quite satisfied having everything a bit scattered and disorganised. The "University of Marriage" strongly suggests that the first few months or even years of any marriage should be spent getting to know, appreciate and accept one another. Applying patience and tolerance for each other's weaknesses will help any couple to find the right balance and compromise.

However, spouses have been known to play the blame game, pointing out faults and insisting on one way or another of doing things rather than giving in or finding a compromise. There is always a Christ-like approach to solving any issues. Some wives, and perhaps even some husbands are known to nag constantly. They complain about anything and everything from morning till night. A nagging woman (or man) can cause a man (or woman) to stay away from home because the home is not a loving castle but a place of irritation and contention.

Better to dwell in the wilderness, than with a contentious and angry woman. (Prov 21:19)

Applying some wisdom can easily solve many issues leading to arguments and naggings. No marriage should end up in a place of no communication or of communication in an argumentative style, because both will invariably lead to mutual resentment, which may ultimately lead to a broken home. It is not necessary to let it go that far, as the "University of Marriage" teaches that open and respectful communication can repair, salvage and improve any relationship.

A soft answer turns away wrath; but a harsh word stirs up anger.(Prov 15:1)

PART III

Practical Tips

1. Short Case Studies

There are many women who have suffered in silence, going through a lot of trauma, not knowing where to turn because society expects them to accept whatever situation they find themselves in and be discreet about it, shameful or not. Some have opened up to me, seeking solutions to their plights. These short case studies will give ideas as to how to handle specific situations that illustrate and inform the lessons of the "University of Marriage" above.

Loss of Income

My husband has lost his job but wants to 'keep up appearances.' I have to maintain the house and he has no regard for me.

When you got married to your husband, you swore to stay by

him no matter what happens, come 'rain or sunshine'. You have been doing well by maintaining the house, however, if he does not have any regard for you, you must do a few things.

- Check your attitude. Have you changed, since you have been maintaining the house? Did it get into your head that you are now playing his role as the head of the household? Are you lording it over him?

- Please do a soul search to see whether you are the problem. Have you tried to see things from his perspective? Have you given it a thought that he may be hiding behind his ego to cover up his shame because as the head of the family he no longer performs his functions? Your husband must be feeling very inadequate right now and would appreciate some understanding even if he doesn't say so.

- God expects you to stand by your man and pray for him, asking for a change in attitude towards you. You must go to God with forgiveness in your heart, a lot of love and a clean mind towards him, and God will answer.

Lack of Family Time

He feels it is important to hang out with his friends for business purposes but it means very little time at home with the family! How should I react? I have no other income.

If you have no other income, your family obviously lives off his work. Staying back with his friends for business purposes means he is still networking for the benefit of his family. However, if you feel left out of these important arrangements, all you need to do is communicate with him.

- God desires that you communicate lovingly with your spouse for a better understanding about your feelings and how to improve your relationship.

- Begin to pray for him to see your point of view by saying it gently and lovingly, not in a confrontational manner.

- A little prayer on your own behalf that enables you to see his point of view helps a great deal as well.

Suspected Infidelity

My husband is frequently travelling for work but I am aware of suspicious emails and texts from women who say that they have spent time with him.

- Are you interested in breaking your marriage or improving on it? Do you want someone else to take your place? If the answers are no, then you need to close your eyes and block your ears. Here's how:

- You must be strong in your inner self to look the other way and turn a deaf ear. For as long as your husband has not told you outright that he doesn't love you anymore, or that he has someone else or that he wants to replace you, there is no reason to look for trouble.

- So long as upon his returns from those countries, he returns to you in your home, there is no real problem. If you begin to kick, rave and rant, he may fight back boldly

to cover up his shame once he discovers that the cat is now out of the bag. If and when he has his back to the wall and knows that you are now aware, he may call your bluff and say "So what! What do you want to do?" What will you do at this point? With all due respect, for as long as your husband is doing everything he does with strange women secretly, it means he still respects you and I do not think you should rock the boat. For if you do, things could deteriorate quickly. About two years ago, a woman felt cheated when she heard a voicemail on her husband's phone after poking her nose into his mobile phone and overheard how a strange woman recounted how she and her husband had a wonderful time.
She held on to the information and they broke up despite having three children caught up in-between.

- Pray for your relationship. A good prayer example is "Lord, let my husband be satisfied with the bosom of the wife of his youth, in Jesus' name, Amen."

Troubled Baggage

I am dealing with a man from a polygamous home. He carries a lot of bad memories from that time and puts constraints on the relationship for this reason.

- There are several likely bad memories your husband could have.

- He may suffer from the insecurity of not knowing what would happen to him, his siblings and his mother if their father suddenly died, because another wife might have more claims on the inheritance than they have.

- He may suffer from the effects of petty jealousies amongst the other wives of his father.

- He may suffer from the fact that his father had to raise many children under a lot of financial constraints meaning they may have had to live in uncomfortable conditions and have developed a phobia for poverty.

- He may suffer from the fact that perhaps his mother and her children were second-class citizens within the larger family and thus were ill-treated.

- Though he may suffer from some of these issues and more, nothing and nobody can say he can't overcome them. His wife must encourage and advise him.

- There is no point in quarrelling over any of the issues. Your husband already has a lot on his mind and he does not need anxieties over his marital relationship to add to his trouble. He needs soothing words of encouragement that tell him that the past is the past and your present relationship will create the future.

- Remind him that there is equality before God amongst His children and that is what matters, not what man thinks or says.

- Your husband has to say 'no' to polygamy in his own nuclear family and not follow the footsteps of his father, otherwise history can and will repeat itself. This also must be drummed into the ears of his sons as they grow up.

Caught Between Modernity and Tradition

I am dealing with a man who cannot decide whether to maintain traditional or more modern beliefs about his role and that of his wife.

With a man who is torn between two ideas for marital bliss, you must apply wisdom and prayer because he cannot change over-night. He must have been brought up in a traditional setting, yet his education and peers have brought him to more modern surroundings, which may have rubbed off on him. His confusion is obvious.

- The Bible says old things have passed away and all things have been made new. Considering that we are living in modern times, in the jet age and not the Stone Age, why would he not move with the times?

- As his wife you should tread softly. Do not force anything on him but keep praying to God to open his eyes. There is nothing the Lord cannot do (Jer. 32:27).

A Childless Marriage

My husband and I have not conceived. I am ready to go through with IVF, yet my husband cannot even consider the fact that he might have a problem. How do we get support from the family?

Why do you feel you have to convince your husband that it may be him who has a fertility problem? The doctors should be able to find out beyond a doubt where the problem lies.

There is no reason why the couple should get the approval of the family once they themselves have decided on the IVF. If anything at all, the family should just be informed.

Lack of Religious Conviction

I believe prayer is the master key but my husband thinks I am fanatical.

- If your husband thinks that you are fanatical about prayer, it may mean that he believes you go overboard with the way you portray your faith. Here are a few ideas to rectify this situation:

- If your husband is not spiritually strong or if he is not really interested in a spiritual journey or if he feels left out, may be you can step back if he is in your presence, but continue praying for him to be able to catch the 'fire' as you have.

- Create enjoyable and meaningful times for family worship, and ever so gently invite him in. Take as many of his suggestions as you possibly can to adjust these prayer sessions to his liking.

Get him to lead the family worship to play his God-given role as the spiritual head of the family.

A Desire for Professional Independence

I want to start my own business but he believes my place is in the home.

Many modern husbands now realise that women can no longer stay at home without a job at hand. Gone are the days when women sit at home idle. Staying at home may be wise for the first few years as the children are born, but later a working woman can help offset the bad state of the economy in our current world. Here are a few arguments that may help convince this particular husband:

- Even if your family is affluent, you will make yourself useful by adding to the family income.

- Since you are passionate about the business, your husband should encourage you because it means you are not lazy. The Bible also talks about the virtuous woman who, despite her busy schedule with her family, still creates time for business to contribute to the success of her family (Prov 31:16)

- Note that you must, however, be able to find a balance between your passion, and your family, so that the home does not suffer.

Homosexuality

My husband is gay. I want to leave but it would set tongues wagging. Also, how do I tell the children?

There is no part of the Bible that says a wife should leave her husband because he is gay. Such men usually hide this deficiency or weakness from their wives but if she does find out, leaving is not the right option. Instead, you should:

- Pray for his deliverance. He may want to stop being gay but can't help himself. Your prayers may help him through the power of Jesus Christ.

- Do not fail in your duty as his wife and remember your vows. If a wife should leave because of the shame the leak would bring, then she would have failed in her duties and vows she took when she got married and said, "For better or worse.... in sickness and in health...." This is a "type of sickness". She would have shirked her responsibilities and God would frown at this. Some end up losing their lives if there is nobody who loves them enough to stick by them.

Abusive Relationships

I am dealing with an abusive husband. Why shouldn't I pour hot water on a man who has so diminished my sense of self through his behaviour, his lies and cheating escapades! How do I turn the other cheek?

I don't think two wrongs make a right. Mean-spirited retaliation will not save any marriage but make it worse. It is not easy to be the abused and scorned wife but a premeditated negative reaction is not the solution. You will only drive your husband further and further away and make him react too, and may do so more violently. So, yes, by all means, turn the other cheek! Here's guidance as to how:

- God appreciates a gentle spirit in women, patience, wisdom and prayer. You must hand your husband to the Lord to break him, melt him, reshape and remould him.

- But first, you have to come to God in love, with no inhibitions and no resentment. You must not harbour any ill will, unforgiving spirit or bitterness. God requires you to change your attitude first before He can do anything about your husband's. Your attitude has to be in His perfect will with all sins removed so that He can answer your prayers. For He is too holy to behold sin.

- You must let God fight for you, and be willing to lose the argument or battle to win the war.

Lack of Love

Why shouldn't I leave the marriage? There are no feelings anymore and he has an "established" relationship with another woman. We don't even share our home anymore. What is wrong with being a divorcee or single lady in Nigeria? The fear of societal backlash and love of the children keeps me locked in a marriage that makes me unhappy.

You may think that your relationship is beyond repair, but it is never too late to try and mend things. With God, all things are possible (Matt. 19:26). But, the real question is, why did you allow your situation to degenerate so badly? You have been allowing agents of darkness to laugh at you. But guess what, you can still get your life back on track.

- Swallow your pride, whether you were right or wrong, humble yourself, and you will bring your marriage back to life.

- Repent (even if you were on the right side all along), because you allowed it to get to this stage before acting.

- Take the matter to the Lord in prayer, seeking His face and ask Him what to do, He will tell you how to appeal to your husband's emotions and how to save your marriage.

Nobody can fix your marriage for you. All anyone can do is help you see what the "University of Marriage" has to offer. The "University of Marriage" teaches from God's book on marriage. It is a good book, a book we should all read and keep reading, a book that can answer most of our questions. But it cannot solve the problems – this is between you, the Holy Spirit and your husband. God will however give you grace in Jesus' name. Amen.

Practical Tips

2. Do's And Don'ts

The "University of Marriage" has lessons to teach every single day of our married life. We are never done learning from each other, never done improving our own conduct within our relationship. The following list of Do's and Don'ts will provide a guideline to acceptable spousal behaviour. Use them as a 'cheat-sheet', as it were, when you take the test of daily-married life.

A Husband's Do's

1. Provide for your family financially; be generous – put their needs first.

2. Appreciate your wife – tell her often that you love her and surprise her with little gifts you know she loves.

3. Love your wife and children unconditionally.

4. Protect, defend, guide and direct your wife and children in whatever they're doing.

5. Praise your wife in her presence; also do so in her absence.

6. Instil discipline lovingly in your children.

7. Show concern and interest about ANY issue that affects your wife and children.

8. Ask for your wife's opinion when making decisions.

9. Take your wife out to functions and on dates.

10. Always treat your wife with respect.

11. Play your role as the spiritual head of the family.

12. Give your wife an allowance not only for the household, but also just for herself, no matter how small.

13. Give your wife adequate attention – spend time with her.

A Husband's Don'ts

1.   Don't neglect your wife nor take her for granted.

2.   Don't abuse your wife – verbally or physically, no matter how angry you may be.

3.   Don't allow your parents and siblings to dictate to your wife or take control in your home.

4.   Don't allow your siblings to live with you, as they would want to interfere and have a say in the workings of your home.

5.   Don't make your wife your slave, even though you're the head of the home.

6.   Never degrade her, particularly not in public.

A Wife's Do's

1. Pray for your husband and family.

2. Love your husband and children unconditionally.

3. Cook your husband's favourite meals often.

4. Keep your home clean and tidy.

5. Make sure there's always food available at home.

6. Keep yourself healthy and beautiful, and your clothing fashionable.

7. Respect your husband and submit to his authority as the head of the home.

8. Run your house efficiently, making sure the needs of your husband and children are met.

9. Have confidence in yourself and your abilities.

10. Train your children to be domesticated and responsible.

11. Be the first to greet your husband every morning.

12. Do your husband's manicure and pedicure regularly.

13. Make sure you are at your husband's beck and call.

14. Wash his clothes or supervise the washing.

15. Apply wisdom in any situation that arises.

16. Always be respectful to your husband.

17. Show him you appreciate him and everything he does for you.

18. Be patient and ready to endure both in good and bad times.

19. Welcome him home warmly.

A Wife's Don'ts

1. Don't nag.

2. Don't neglect the family.

3. Don't belittle or embarrass your husband by correcting him in public.

4. Don't look for trouble: don't keep suspecting him and searching his pockets or phones to check for messages that might prove adultery.

5. Don't taunt him if he's unable to meet his obligations to you and your family, especially when it is not his fault (such as when he loses his job).

6. Look the other way when necessary or possible to avoid quarrels and arguments with him.

Mutual Do's

1. Be faithful to your spouse.

2. Kiss and hug your spouse daily as physical contact encourages closeness.

3. Pray together.

4. Settle your disputes without involving others.

5. Treat your better half with respect.

6. Don't listen to rumours.

7. Always accept lovemaking advances from your spouse.

8. Apologise and forgive each other when you have hurt one another.

9. Keep the lines of communication open at all times. Always listen and be ready to talk when your partner has something to say.

11. Encourage and lift each other up when things go wrong.

12. Confide in each other and don't keep secrets.

13. Share the same bed and try to avoid king size beds so that tight quarters will keep you close.

14. Control your tongue even when provoked or when tempted to say hurtful words.

15. Be sure to give each other good and honest advice when necessary.

16. Be tolerant and patient when dealing with each other.

Mutual Don'ts

1. Don't keep malice.

2. Don't keep records of each other's wrongdoings.

3. Don't have separate bedrooms.

4. Don't report your spouse's wrongdoings to your friends and family; report to God instead.

5. Don't allow your parents and siblings to mediate in your affairs.

6. Don't stay angry with your partner – don't let the sun go down without making up with each other.

7. Don't compare your spouse to those of your friends – each person is a unique individual.

8. Don't do things you cannot admit to your spouse.

3. Matriculation Without Graduation: A Lifelong Journey in Marriage and Prayer

A lot has been said about how spouses should react to one another when faced with challenges. However, many may find it difficult to put these suggestions into practice. The Holy Spirit, from personal and practical experience and from counselling sessions, has combined them from revelations. In other words, these suggestions, tips and ideas are tried and true. Follow them, and your marital relationship will improve.

This is God's will. For God does not want any marriage to break up, unless there is no more hope. But hope does not disappoint because Christ Jesus has poured out His love in our hearts.

Yet before we can decide that there is no hope for our relationship, we must consult with God in prayer. If we do so with a genuine heart, there is nothing He is not willing to listen to. He is our heavenly Father who loves us more than our earthly parents; He is always willing to do what's best for us. In return we must strive for there to be less of us and more of Him in all we do. When we are struggling with life's issues, especially in our marriage, He is always willing to deliver us.

Yet we must always remember that there are many issues to consider when thinking of divorce or separation, such as:

- What happened to the vows that we have said before God?

- What happens to the spiritual covering of the man over the woman?

- Is it a wise step?

- Will it really bring improvement or happiness in your life?

- How do you maintain your life-style or your home?

The Holy Spirit will bring up all these questions, and more, in the mind of each troubled partner in calmer moments. The answers usually point towards staying together and trying to save the marriage. God does not really want any marriage to breakup, unless it is a life-threatening situation for either partner.

Marriage, like life, is a university where there is matriculation and education but no graduation. There are 'ups' and 'downs', and as much as 'ups' are often followed by 'downs', any 'down' promises an 'up'. Therefore we should not light-heartedly walk away from a union that was made in God's presence. Marriage, like life, is a continuous process.

There are seven main tools that, if applied, will form a solid foundation for a marriage to build upon and grow:

- Love

- Prayer

- Wisdom and understanding

- Patience

- Submission

- Communication

- Obedience

A home built on the Lord Jesus, nurtured by a virtuous woman with a God-fearing responsible man, both spending time to be there for one another and their children, will stand strong in the storms of life like a house built on a rock (Matt. 7:24).

As husband and wife pray for one another, miracles happen as the hardness of hearts melt away, forgiveness takes the place of all the pain and suffering they may have caused each other. As we enter God's presence in prayer for others, especially our spouse, God fills our hearts with His love, and it is His love that grows within us for our spouse. Even if our partner is not there, he or she will automatically reciprocate and begin to love you back.

Now, let us pray:

Lord Jesus, I pray for my wife:

Lord, I plead that You would create in her a love that will endure the stress and problems that we might face in this marriage. (1 Cor 13:4-7)

Lord, I ask that she would not be rude or thoughtless towards me. (1 Cor 13:5)

God, I plead that she will share my burdens and hurts. (1 Cor 13:5)

Father, I plead that she would be faithful and attend and serve in Your church. (Heb 10:25)

Lord, please make my wife a virtuous woman. (Prov 31:10-31)

Lord, instil Your fear in my wife to overcome sexual temptation and immorality. (1 Cor 6:18-20)

Lord Jesus, I pray for my husband:

God, create within my husband a hunger for me and our children. Let him find satisfaction in me. (Prov 5:19-20)

Lord, I plead that You would give him a heart to seek after You and serve You all the days of his life. (Ps 63:1)

Father, I pray that You would grant him the wisdom and power to gain and use his finances wisely. (Prov 3:9-10)

Lord, I ask that You would deliver him from petty and resentful thoughts in our relationship. (Matt 18:20-21)

Father, help him to discern and deal with those things that hinder and hurt our relationship. (Ps 139:23-24)

Father, grant that he might find great delight and joy in me. (Prov 5:18)

Lord, give my husband a new wife, but let it be me in Jesus' name. Amen.

Dear Lord, let my husband be faithful and loyal to our children and I.

Father, let my husband make wise decisions which will affect our children and I positively.

Father, I thank you for the lives of your children, and I join my faith with theirs in agreement believing and trusting that you have answered all these prayers in Jesus name. Amen.

From now on, we shall live together in deep love, relying on Your word and promises for a fruitful life with our children seated around our tables like olive trees in Jesus' mighty name. Amen.

Index

Index

Index

Index

Index

Index

Index

Index

About the Author

Mrs. Folorunso Alakija is a philanthropist with a sincere desire to help the needy, a fashion icon with an infallible sense of style, a businesswoman who has broken many uncharted territories, a friend in deed, a loving wife, a caring mother and grandmother. Educated in Europe, she first embarked on a career in banking, until she took a leap of faith and followed her heart and creative calling to establish her own business in the Nigerian fashion industry. Supreme Stitches rose to prominence and fame within a few years, and, as Rose of Sharon House of Fashion, became a household name.

As National President and lifelong Trustee of the Fashion Designers Association of Nigeria (FADAN), she left an indelible mark, promoting Nigerian Culture through fashion and style.

Ever the entrepreneur, Mrs. Alakija has forayed into related businesses: The Rose of Sharon Prints & Promotions specialises in monogramming and screen printing for promotional and gift items, while Digital Reality Print Ltd. specialises in highly technical digital large format printing. She remains the only female in that industry to date. She has just included a direct imaging paper printing press to coincide with her 60th birthday. She oversees the Rose of Sharon Group as the Group Managing Director and she is also Executive Vice Chairman of her family's oil exploration and production business.

Looking back on a lifetime of achievements, Folorunso's foremost desire is to give glory to God and to share the secret of her success. A Christian since 1991, she draws her strength from her unfaltering belief in the power and glory of God. In a sincere desire to give to those in need in the name of the Lord, her philanthropic endeavors, such as the Rose of Sharon Foundation, continue to positively influence her native land by empowering widows and their families as well as orphans to be successful through educational programmes and scholarships.

At 60, Mrs. Alakija oversees her businesses and philanthropic enterprises working tirelessly with boundless energy, and follows her evangelical calling with unbridled devotion, hoping to inspire the younger generation with her motto " whatever is worth doing at all is worth doing well.

She lives in Lagos, Nigeria with Modupe Alakija her beloved husband of 35 years, and their four sons and grandchild.

Other Titles by the Author

"The author must be highly commended for putting a lot of time, memories, effort and research collating the information in this book, which is a must read for everyone.

Her keen sense of perfection, strong family ties, religious commitment, love of God and people could have been part of the driving force in the production of such a masterpiece. This book would help any reader to rediscover himself."

Chief Mrs Leila Fowler
Proprietress and Founder Vivian Fowler Memorial College for Girls

"She [Folorunso Alakija] was very much part of the International Merchant Bank of Nigeria Ltd (IMB) that transformed banking in Nigeria and produced the modern generation of bankers that have placed Nigeria on the global map... Mrs.

Folorunso Alakija is certainly gifted and born to succeed. She takes everything to perfection. No wonder she is the star she is today in her family and professional careers. She is an inspiration that affects us all."

HRM Ebitimi E.Banigo, OFR
Okpo XXI of Okpoma Kingdom, Bayelsa,
Chairman of the Board, FAAN

"She has always been a very good friend, confidant and big sister. When I am with her, I can speak truthfully about anything and I know I am not judged. Mrs. Folorunso Alakija is a generous astute businesswoman, who loves God in totality, a devoted wife, mother and a philanthropist par excellence."

Chief (Mrs.) Oluremi Tinubu, OON
Senator, Lagos Central Senatorial District

"A most fascinating read by a truly inspirational icon. A definite bestseller."

Ancorapoint Ltd.